Police Officer Exam Prep

2021-2022

Study Guide + 300 Questions and Detailed Answer Explanations (Includes 4 Full-Length Practice Tests)

Table of Contents

Background Information

The Police Officer Selection Test (POST) is a basic skills test conducted by the police department to select the most qualified applicants as entry-level officers. Through this test, the department is able to ensure that its officers possess the basic skills they need to excel in their chosen career.

This test is specifically designed to test an applicant's cognitive skills in four areas: mathematics, grammar, reading comprehension, and incident report writing. Applicants who pass this test are in pole position to get their dream job, as opposed to their counterparts who fail the test.

Many county, municipal, state, and federal government law enforcement agencies use the POST test for officer selection. Currently, some 30 state police chief associations across the United States use the examination for recruiting new police officers.

The written test is the first stage of the recruitment process. If you pass the examination, the police department will place you on its eligibility list for subsequent evaluation. Your selection is dependent on your performance. Hence, the higher your score on the test, the better your chances of being shortlisted for further evaluation.

Police agencies do not all conduct the same test. The test varies across agencies, and some agencies do not conduct the test themselves but outsource it to third parties. Thus, aside from your examination results, another factor that will determine your selection is the agency conducting your examination, since these agencies have their own individual basis for selection.

General Section

The general section covers some important areas of the test and pieces of information that will assist you both before and during the test.

Test Format

The Police Officer Selection Test is divided into four sections. These are mathematics, reading comprehension, grammar, and incident report writing. The first three sections are multiple-choice questions while the fourth section, incident report writing, requires you to write out your answers in the provided space. The answers must be complete sentences, grammatically correct, and without spelling errors.

How to Register for the Exam

Registering for the examination is not challenging. You may visit the local police agency you want to join and make inquiries about the registration process. However, since the police departments in most states have official websites, you may visit their website and get the necessary registration information from there. Then, you can proceed with the registration with the available information.

Duration and Cost of the Test

The four-part test will take about 1 hour, 15 minutes and costs $35.

Examination Tips

In addition to studying for the examination, preparing yourself physically for the examination is crucial to your success. For a couple of days before the examination, it is advisable to steer clear of junk food. Instead, eat a balanced diet to boost your physical fitness.

Stimulants and tranquilizers must be avoided too. On the test day, do not drink coffee. If you must drink a hot beverage, tea is better. Try to get as much sleep as you can the night before. Staying up until a few hours before the examination will be counterproductive.

If you drink alcohol, put off that habit for the couple of days leading up to the examination. On no condition should you drink alcohol before the test. Alcohol may impede your performance and cause you to fail.

Watch what you eat on the day of your exam. Go for a light meal over a heavy one. Drink water or any other liquid in moderation to reduce your frequency of restroom visits.

Communicate with your peers when preparing for the test. If you know someone who has already taken the test, you could gain some valuable information or tips to get ahead.

Join relevant social media groups. Who knows, you may find groups or pages designed for sharing information and tips on passing the test. Some may share their experiences, including successes and failures. From the successful individuals, learn practical tips that can help you to ace the test. Also learn from those who failed the test. If there are mistakes you can avoid, steer clear of them to increase your chances of passing the examination.

You should also identify your strengths and weaknesses. Are you good in mathematics but poor in grammar? Identifying your weaknesses and strengths will enable you to identify areas where you must improve if you desire to pass. Without this knowledge, you may be preparing blindly for the examination and eventually fail it.

Schedule your studying as soon as you can to give yourself ample time and opportunity to prepare extensively for the test. If you are already working, design your study schedule to maximize the little time you can afford. A good study schedule should help you spread your study time at your convenience. Thus, you will end up studying for a specific hour every day, rather than waiting until a couple of days before the examination and cramming it in then.

Time management is crucial to your success on the test. The importance of arriving on time cannot be overemphasized. During the test, time management is also vital. Remember that the examination time is set. So, make sure you understand the allotted time for each section and endeavor to do as much as you can within the allotted time.

Set aside a few minutes to go through your answer booklet before submission. Do not be in a hurry to submit your script and leave the examination center until you are absolutely sure that you have done everything perfectly well. The short amount of time you devote to cross-checking your answers could mean the difference between success and failure.

For the grammar section, spend enough time in advance honing your skills. This section is pretty broad and covers many topics, such as parts of speech, punctuation, sentence structure, and concord, among others. The more you learn about these parts of grammar, the more competent you will become at answering questions on them. Do not forget to learn as much as you can about homophones, frequently misspelled words, and common grammatical errors. This knowledge will come in handy while answering the questions.

How to Prepare for the Examination

To begin your preparation for the examination, check with the local police department you want to apply for. The police department will furnish you with the necessary information you will need for the exam. Then, start your preparation.

You probably understand the importance of adequate preparation for an examination of this magnitude. Thus, as soon as you get this book, go through each section as many times as you need to grasp its content.

The questions and answers sections are designed to help you remember everything you have learned from the guide. Answer these questions as accurately as possible. Once you are done, compare your answers with those provided for each section. Your performance will determine how much information you are able to recollect while studying the guide. It will also determine how much effort you still need to put into your preparation to be fully prepared for the examination. Stop practicing only when you can confidently answer the questions in the book.

To get the best out of this guide, develop a practical study routine and stick to it. Depending on your schedule and how quickly you learn, you can set aside an hour a day for reading and testing your comprehension. If you have a friend or family member who wants to take the examination as well, you may want to share ideas with them.

You can make the preparation section fun and informative by turning it into a game. Test your math skills by solving math problems without the aid of a calculator. The more you do this, the better you will become at math. Gradually, you will increase your chances of performing well in the selection exam.

Start your preparation for the test as soon you decide to take the test. Do not wait until a few days or weeks before the examination before you start preparing. The earlier you start, the easier it will be to adequately prepare for the test. Otherwise, if you wait until the eleventh hour, you may not cover enough material needed for the examination. You may also be tempted to cram as much material as you can, which will be counterproductive. While cramming is seemingly beneficial, it will actually interfere with your comprehension. That may undermine your efforts and lead to a substandard performance on the test.

Time Limits

Each section has its own time limit. The mathematics section contains 20 questions. You have 20 minutes to attempt all the questions. The reading comprehension section contains 25 questions. You have 1 minute to attempt each question. Grammar and incident report writing have 20 and 10 questions, respectively. Nevertheless, 15 minutes is allotted to each section. In all, you have 1 hour, 15 minutes to attempt the 75 questions on the examination.

In view of the allotted time for each section, ensure that you do not get held up on difficult questions. That is a waste of time. Rather, attempt the ones you are familiar with first. If you still have time to spare, revisit the tough ones and see if you can crack them. You will not be penalized for wrong answers. Thus, you can guess answers to tough questions to increase your chances of scoring a higher mark on the exam.

How to Mark Your Answers

Since this is a computer-scored examination, you must endeavor to mark your answers correctly. Poorly marked answers may lead to a low score, as the computer may be unable to decide whether your answers are correct or not.

It is advisable that you use a soft lead pencil, such as #2. Ink is forbidden. When marking the corresponding answer, ensure that you mark the oval with black marks that can be easily identified by the computer. If you wish to change an answer, erase the wrong answer completely before marking another oval. If you do not, the computer may identify two marks for a question and mark it as incorrect. Bear this in mind when handling multiple-choice questions.

What You Can Do

Before the commencement of the examination, the administrator will provide you with instructions for each section. You should pay attention to the test administrator while they provide the detailed instructions because these differ from one section to another. If you miss a piece of information, ask the administrator to kindly repeat it. Do not dismiss it—every piece of information counts.

Preparation in advance of the examination is a necessity. With the aid of this guide, you can gain an idea of how the examination will go and be prepared for it.

Composure is a virtue during the exam. Regardless of what is going on around you or in your mind, maintain a sense of calm. Although the exam may make you nervous, do not betray your emotions. If you can get your emotions under control, you will be emotionally ready for the examination.

What You Cannot Do

Do not arrive late to the examination center. Being punctual will help you get used to the environment before you start. You can settle down properly and be in the right frame of mind for the exam. Conversely, lateness to the center may disqualify you.

More so, when you are punctual, you can enjoy the luxury of choosing your own seat or being assigned a comfortable place. You will miss out on this privilege if you arrive at the examination center at the last minute. You may consider sitting in the front row. This makes you noticeable to the proctors who double as members of the selection list.

Do not bring foreign materials into the center except those allowed by the examination body. Your mobile device, smartwatch, and other personal effects are forbidden from the exam hall. It is recommended that you keep these in a safe place if you cannot leave them at home.

Cheating in any form is also forbidden. Having a discussion with a fellow candidate during the examination will earn you an automatic disqualification. Under no circumstances should you look at another candidate's paper.

Do not converse in a loud voice with other candidates before the exam commences. Once the proctor starts their address, all forms of conversation are forbidden. Wearing overly casual clothing is frowned upon. Wear the appropriate attire for the examination to avoid disqualification.

Where to Take the Test

The local policy academy you want to register with will provide you with all the information you will need about the examination, including the location of the test center. Ensure you have this information in advance before the actual exam day. Note that the examination is conducted in municipalities, cities, towns, and other places where a police agency exists.

How Many Times Can You Retake the Test?

The agency in question determines the frequency of the test. Therefore, this is another important piece of information you need to obtain from your agency when you make contact.

With this information in mind and plenty of practice from the rest of this book, you will have all you need to approach the exam with confidence and pass with flying colors.

Chapter One: Mathematics

This section of the examination tests your ability to perform some basic arithmetic as a police officer. Hence, we will look at some basic arithmetic such as addition, subtraction, multiplication, and division.

Fractions

In a fraction, the upper number is referred to as the numerator, while the lower number, the denominator. A typical example of a fraction is 3/4 where 3 and 4 are the numerator and denominator, respectively.

Types of Fractions

Fractions can exist in three forms. These are proper fractions, improper fractions, and mixed fractions. A proper fraction is a type of fraction in which the numerator is smaller than the denominator, whereas an improper fraction has a numerator larger than its denominator. Examples of proper and improper fractions, respectively, are 4/7 and 9/4.

A mixed fraction contains two elements. These are a whole number and a fractional part, which is usually a proper fraction. An example of a mixed fraction is $2\frac{4}{7}$, where 2 is the whole number part and 4/7 is the proper fraction part.

Fraction-to-Decimal Conversion

A fraction can be converted to a decimal by dividing the numerator by the denominator. The division is done until the numerator is completely divided without a remainder.

Example 1

Let us say that 4/5 of the police personnel in a state are in the Special Force. Convert this figure to a decimal.

Solution:
$$5 \overline{)4.{}^{4}0} = 0.8$$

Find the number of times that 5 can divide into 4.

Since 5 is greater than 4, 5 cannot divide into 4. Hence, the answer is 0.

Since there is no other number after 4, add 0 to it to make 4.0.

How many times can 5 divide into 40? The answer is 8.

Thus, 4/5 is 0.8.

Example 2

A gang of kidnappers increased their operations by 3/2 of the original value over the past five years. What is that fraction in decimal form?

Solution:

$$\begin{array}{r} 1.5 \\ 2\overline{\smash{)}3.{}^{1}0} \end{array}$$

Find the number of times that 2 can divide into 3. The answer is 1, with remainder 1.

Since there is no other number after 3, add a 0 to make it 3.0.

Carry the remainder 1 to this 0 to become 10.

How many times can 2 divide into 10? The answer is 5.

Hence, the kidnappers have increased their operations by 1.5 times.

Example 3

Convert $1\frac{3}{4}$ to a decimal.

This is the conversion of a mixed fraction to a decimal.

Leave the whole-number part.

Convert the fractional part to a decimal.

$$\begin{array}{r} 0.7\ 5 \\ 4\overline{\smash{)}3.{}^{3}0\ {}^{2}0} \end{array}$$

How many times can 4 divide 3? The answer is 0.

Add a 0 to make it 3.0 and carry the 3 to this 0 to become 30.

Find the number of times that 4 can divide into 30. The answer is 7, remainder 2.

Add another 0, then carry the remainder 2 to the 0 to become 20.

Find the number of times that 4 can divide into 20. The answer is 5 exactly.

To find the final answer, add the whole number to the result of the 3/4 conversion.

= 1 + 0.75 = 1.75.

Therefore, $1\frac{3}{4}$ is 1.75 in decimal form.

Decimal-to-Fraction Conversion

Just as you can convert fractions to decimals, decimal-to-fraction conversion is also possible. The process is the reverse of the fraction-to-decimal conversion. Some examples are shown below:

Example 1

If 0.6 of the sum of money in a cash register was stolen by a team of robbers, what fraction of the money in the cash register was stolen?

Solution:

Write out the decimal as a whole number.

The decimal is 0.6, which becomes 6 when it is *multiplied* by 10.

Therefore 0.6 is the same as 6 *divided* by 10.

Or 6/10

Now that we have a fraction, this can be reduced to its lowest terms.

What number can divide into both the numerator (6) and denominator (10)?

Since they are both multiples of 2, 2 can divide into them both.

Divide both the numerator and denominator by 2.

Hence, 6/10 = 3/5

Therefore, 3/5 of the money in the cash register was stolen.

Example 2

A kidnapper returned 0.75 of the ransom he collected from his victim before he was apprehended. What fraction of the ransom did he return?

Solution:

Write out the decimal as a whole number.

The fractional part is 0.75, which becomes 75 when it is *multiplied* by 100.

Therefore, 0.75 is the same as 75 *divided* by 100.

Or 75/100

Now that we have a fraction, this can be reduced to its lowest terms.

In this case, we can divide 75 and 100 by 25.

75/100 = 3/4

Therefore, the kidnapper has returned 3/4 of the ransom.

Example 3

The police have successfully solved 0.5 of the woman-trafficking cases reported to them over the last six months. What fraction of the cases have been solved?

Solution:

Write out the decimal as a whole number.

The decimal is 0.5, which becomes 5 when it is *multiplied* by 10.

Therefore, 0.5 is the same as 5 *divided* by 10.

Or 5/10

When reduced, 5/10 = 1/2.

Therefore, the police have successfully solved 1/2 of all woman-trafficking cases over the last six months.

Percentages

Numbers are said to be expressed as a percentage when they are expressed relative to 100. It is noteworthy that both decimal numbers and fractions can be expressed as a percentage. You can also find the percentage of other integers aside from fractions and decimals.

Example 1

Four out of every 5 domestic abuse victims are women. What percentage of domestic abuse victims are women?

Solution:

To turn any fraction into a percentage, we multiply by 100.

To calculate $4/5 \times 100$:

Step 1: Multiply 4 by 100.

Step 2: Divide by 5.

$4 \times 100 = 400$

$400/5 = 80$

Therefore, 80% of domestic abuse victims are women.

Alternatively, you can switch the steps. Divide 4 by 5 first.

$4/5 = 0.8$

Multiply the result by 100.

$0.8 \times 100 = 80$

Thus, 80% of domestic abuse victims are women.

Example 2

Jane spends $2,500 monthly. She spends $2,000 on personal expenses and saves $500. What percentage of her expenses does she save?

Solution:

Total expenses: $2,500

Savings: $500

$500 out of $2,500 as a fraction is 500/2,500.

To turn any fraction into a percentage, we multiply by 100.

500/2500 × 100

Step 1: Multiply 500 by 100.

Step 2: Divide by 2,500.

500 × 100 = 50,000

50,000/2,500 = 20

Therefore, $500 is 20% of $2,500.

Note that you can also solve any of these percentage problems by first converting the numbers to decimals before multiplying them by 100. You will still arrive at the same answer.

For instance, to express 4 as a percentage of 5, first convert 4/5 to a decimal.

4/5 = 0.8

0.8 × 100 = 80

Hence, 4 is 80% of 5.

You can solve the second question using this technique to confirm the method's accuracy.

Example 3

A man spends $400 out of his income on gas. He spends another $1,200 on insurance. If the man's income is $4,000, what percentage of his income does he spend on gas?

Solution:

Income amount: $4,000

Amount spent on gas: $400

To find the percentage of his income he spends on gas, divide the amount spent on gas by the income amount.

Amount spent on gas/income amount = $400/$4,000

$400/$4,000 is the fraction that is gas, but the large numbers are difficult to deal with.

$400 is a multiple of both. So, divide through by $400 to make the calculation easier.

($400/$400) / ($4,000/$400) = 1/10 or 0.1

Now that you have a simple decimal, you can multiply it by 100 to turn it into a percentage.

0.1 × 100 = 10

Hence, the man spends 10% of his income on gas.

Fraction-to-Percentage Conversion

Once you are familiar with fractions, you can do this conversion with ease. Simply divide the numerator by the denominator, then multiply the resulting decimal by 100.

Example 1

Of the people living in a crime-infested area, 5/7 have been exposed to robbery and assault. What percentage of the populace are victims of robbery and assault?

Solution:

To convert this value to a percentage, first divide the numerator by the denominator. Then, multiply the result by 100.

Thus, 5/7 = 0.7143

Try to calculate more than two decimal places (as above) to ensure your answer is accurate.

Multiply 0.7143 by 100:

0.7143 × 100 = 71.43

Hence, 71.43% of the populace has at one time or another experienced robbery and assault.

Example 2

Only 20 out of 35 applicants into the police academy were admitted. What percentage of the applicants were admitted?

Solution:

Divide the numerator by the denominator and then multiply the result by 100.

20/35 = 4/7 in lowest terms

4/7 = 0.5714

Multiply 0.5714 by 100.

0.5714 × 100 = 57.14

Thus, 57.14% of the applicants were admitted into the police academy.

Example 3

Only two-fifths of a robber's loot was ever recovered. Convert the recovered loot to a percentage.

Solution:

Two-fifths = 2/5

Divide the numerator by the numerator to turn it into a decimal.

2/5 = 0.4

Multiply the result by 100.

$0.4 \times 100 = 40$

Therefore, 40% of the loot was recovered.

Decimal-to-Percentage Conversion

Decimal-to-percentage conversion is unarguably the simplest form of percentage conversion. You only need to multiply the decimal number by 100 and you are done.

Example 1

If 0.23 of the citizens of a country have criminal tendencies, what percentage of the citizens have criminal tendencies?

Solution:

Multiply the decimal equivalent of people with criminal tendencies by 100.

$0.23 \times 100 = 23$

Therefore, 23% of the citizens are inclined toward crime.

Example 2

A research report shows that 0.0056 of people living in slums are exposed to one crime or another before they become teenagers. What percentage of people living in slums have such an experience before becoming teenagers?

Solution:

Multiply the decimal value by 100.

$0.0056 \times 100 = 0.56$

Hence, 0.56% of the people have such an experience before becoming teenagers.

Example 3

Of the inmates of a particular prison, 0.4 are convicted of money laundering. Express this as a percentage of the total number of inmates in the prison.

Solution:

Multiply the given value by 100.

$0.4 \times 100 = 40$

Therefore, 40% of the inmates are convicted of money laundering.

These are the topics you will come across in the mathematics section. Be familiar with these topics to increase your chances of performing well on the exam.

Chapter Two: Reading Comprehension

Reading comprehension is a skill you must develop while preparing for the Police Officer Selection Test. While you need this skill for the POST examination, you equally need it as a police officer. If your reading comprehension ability is nothing to write home about, you are setting yourself up for failure in the examination. You must bring it up to par to get the desired result on the test.

If you are looking to improve your reading comprehension ability, this section will address some comprehension-related issues, such as reading comprehension challenges, signs of reading comprehension challenges, and causes of reading comprehension challenges. It also provides some comprehension tips.

Reading Comprehension Challenges

Not everyone is endowed with comprehension ability. Some people struggle with this problem, as they find it difficult to identify the main ideas in any given text. The problem will have a negative impact on their performance when preparing for examinations or generally reading a material.

Sadly, not everyone with a reading comprehension challenge is aware of this problem. They consider it a minor issue that can just be dismissed. However, the opposite is the case. If you are struggling with reading, you must work on fixing this problem if you desire a career on the police force.

For instance, your job description may include reading reports, drawing inferences from a report, or engaging in tasks that will test your reading comprehension skills. Thus, it is imperative to know whether you are struggling with reading comprehension or not.

Signs of Reading Comprehension Challenges

If you are unsure whether you have comprehension challenges or not, go through the following signs of reading comprehension challenges and see if you identify with any of them.

The inability to identify the main ideas in a document you are reading indicates a struggle with comprehension. People who are lost while reading usually cannot make head or tail of the content. Hence, they find comprehension difficult.

Another sign of a reading comprehension challenge is the inability to answer questions regarding a reading material. If you understand a text, you will not struggle to answer questions that are drawn from the passage. However, if you are always distracted or have poor vocabulary, the chances are you will not be able to easily comprehend the text and will struggle to answer any questions regarding it.

People who usually lose interest while reading also have issues with comprehension. Their failure to understand what they are reading is one of the factors behind their loss of interest. Hence, if you cannot sustain interest in a material you are reading, you may be struggling with comprehension.

Another indicator of a reading comprehension problem is struggling to narrate a story or summarize material you just read. It goes without saying that if you are familiar with a document and understand the content, expressing the thoughts and ideas in it in your own words should not be too challenging. Narrating to your friends or family a story you just read should not be stressful if you understand the story. Hence, if you are unable to give a summary of a document or share the lessons in a story with others, you may have comprehension issues.

In written material, you may come across new words, phrases, and grammatical elements. If they sound unfamiliar to you and you cannot guess their meaning from their context, that is a sign that you are not comfortable with reading comprehension.

Poor reading habits are another sign of reading comprehension issues. If you struggle with reading, you will find comprehension challenging. Some signs of poor reading include skipping words, substituting one word for another, and other related poor reading habits.

If you skip words while reading, the sentence containing the skipped words will become meaningless to you. Substituting one word for another has the same outcome. This is common among people who cannot differentiate between homophones. Substituting *son* for *sun* in a sentence, or vice versa, will bury the idea contained in the sentence. That will hurt your comprehension.

Some people can read aloud fluently but have zero idea of what they have just read. If you have a similar experience, this may indicate comprehension issues.

If you display any of the signs discussed above, it is advisable that you work on improving your comprehension ability. However, before you do that, find out the common causes of your comprehension challenges and identify which is probably responsible for your inability to easily understand a study material.

Causes of Reading Comprehension Challenges

Several factors can trigger reading difficulty. A couple of these factors are discussed below:

Grammatical and linguistic incompetence: People who are grammatically sound have zero issues with comprehension. Such individuals are familiar with rules of grammar, semantics, syntax, and other elements of grammar that aid comprehension. Thus, their comprehension is strong even with difficult texts. If you are not competent grammatically, you may have comprehension issues.

Academic background: Your academic background may affect your comprehension ability. If you have a very sound academic background, you will not find comprehension challenging. The same cannot be said for someone from a poor academic background. Their lack of exposure to reading will have a significant effect on their comprehension levels.

It goes without saying that if you were not accustomed to reading in childhood, picking up a reading habit as an adult may be difficult. Even if you do, you need a substantial amount of effort to overcome the limitations posed by a poor academic background and improve your reading and comprehension skills.

Learning disability: Some learning disabilities like dyslexia and coexisting disorders such as attention-deficit/hyperactivity disorder (ADHD) are common causes of reading problems. ADHD is known for its negative effect on concentration, which can make reading comprehension more challenging.

On the other hand, dyslexia sufferers experience reading *difficulty*. They struggle with word pronunciation and other challenges that hinder smooth reading. The end result is a lack of understanding of what they struggled to read.

No motivation: A lack of motivation is another reason why a lot of people have issues with comprehension. They see no reason why they should put in the effort to understand a reading material, especially if the material is boring or if they have no previous knowledge of the material's subject.

Without seeing a tangible reason to devote your time and energy to reading a document, your primary goal of reading and understanding it may be automatically defeated before you even start. It is an entirely different ball game if you *are* motivated to read.

Lack of concentration: A short attention span ranks high among the several factors behind poor comprehension. Many people, even with the best intentions, cannot sustain their reading concentration for long. They may start well, but they end up losing concentration a couple of minutes into reading and thus lose out on the opportunity to read and understand a text.

Sources of distraction abound today more than ever. From the allure of social media to binge-watching Netflix, several things fight for your attention simultaneously. If you cannot put these distractions aside, you will lose the concentration you need to read and understand a text.

Limited vocabulary: Your vocabulary is another determinant of comprehension ability. A sentence may contain several elements of grammar. Your degree of understanding of these elements will go a long way in determining your comprehension. For instance, if you come across idioms or phrasal verbs you have no idea about, you will struggle to understand the full sentence.

Limited vocabulary may affect your reading and comprehension in another way. If you have to look up a new word each time you come across one, you may run out of desire to continue reading, especially if it has taken a substantial amount of your time. Hence, poor or limited vocabulary may affect your reading and comprehension in several ways.

Poor reading technique: You are not limited to a single reading technique. You can choose a convenient reading technique from the avalanche of options at your disposal. Your choice may determine your comprehension level. If you adopt the wrong technique, you may not find comprehension easy. Conversely, the right strategy that suits you should boost your understanding level.

Difficulty with word recognition is another factor that may hinder your comprehension. If you cannot recognize the words that make up phrases and clauses in a sentence, understanding the sentence is impossible. Thus, difficulty with word recognition will have a massive effect on your reading and comprehension skills.

The above are a handful of causes of poor reading comprehension. Once you identify the factor(s) behind your poor comprehension, you can take steps to fix the problem and thus become better at understanding any given material.

Reading Comprehension Skills

While the above problems may hinder your comprehension ability, you can overcome the challenge and take your comprehension skills to the next level. Developing the following skills will help you put these challenges behind you and master the art of reading comprehension.

First, improve your vocabulary. Learn new words, phrases, idioms, and phrasal verbs regularly. The knowledge will prove useful when you come across such expressions while reading. You should also endeavor to learn the synonyms, antonyms, and homophones of new words so that you will not find it difficult to understand such words when you come across them.

The meanings of words are not limited to their literal meanings. A word's context may influence its meaning, and your ability to understand a word contextually plays a huge role in your comprehension. Hence, while learning word meanings, pay attention to their context within sentences. This will widen the scope of your knowledge and help improve your comprehension ability.

Understanding the organizational structure of a sentence is also crucial to understanding its content. Hence, your efforts to improve your comprehension skills should not be limited to learning only individual words. It should also include understanding how sentences are structured. Your efforts will pay off as you gradually overcome your comprehension obstacle.

Reading Comprehension Strategies

There are several comprehension-boosting strategies that you can use to improve your reading. Here are some common options:

Annotate texts: Annotating texts is a brilliant way to improve your comprehension skills. When annotating a text, identify some main points in a study material and write them beside the material. You can also do extra research on the subject and jot the extra information you learn beside the material. This improves your understanding of the subject matter.

Similar to annotating is note taking. You may pay attention to important details or ideas in a study material and make note of them in a jotter or other writing material. Note taking and annotating offer the same benefit. You have something you can always use as a reminder of the main ideas in whatever you read. Having this will boost your comprehension level.

Practice PQ4R: PQ4R is an effective reading comprehension strategy that anyone can employ. Each letter represents a different strategy for boosting your comprehension.

The P stands for Preview and the Q for Question, while the 4R stands for Read, Reflect, Recite, and Review. How can you implement these strategies to boost your comprehension ability?

The first step is to preview a document before reading it. To preview given material, first scan the text for the overall message. Knowing the author's primary message will aid your understanding when you read the text more thoroughly later. You should also try to determine whether the text is written for academic purposes, pleasure reading, or any other purpose.

While previewing a document, check the prologue and conclusion. Pay attention to chapters and subheadings as well. You may uncover some hidden gems from these sections.

Next, question the material. Your questions should be designed to draw out the main ideas. Ask yourself what message the author is trying to send to you. What is the primary objective? How does the context support the overall message? Asking these and other related questions will boost your understanding of the text.

Reading the material comes next. While reading thoroughly, focus on getting answers to the questions you previously asked. This requires you to pay attention to every detail. Paying rapt attention will improve your assimilation rate and generally boost your comprehension skills.

During and after reading the material, you should reflect on what you read. This will help you absorb the material and clarify the main points. Thus, you should pause at intervals to meditate or reflect on what you are reading. So, reading the entire material in one go should not be your ultimate goal. Instead, your goal should be *understanding* it as you go along.

Next, recite the material. Your reading should not be limited to reading and reflecting only. Recite the important points out loud to make them sink deeper. This exercise is crucial for retaining a greater portion of what you learn from the material.

The final step is review. After completing the previous steps, review everything you learned so far. Go through your notes and annotations during the review process. Revising the highlighted points will jog your memory and help you remember the main points. That is the essence of comprehension.

Leverage context clues: Leveraging context clues is another comprehension strategy to help overcome whatever challenges may stand between you and reading comprehension.

The context of a word refers to the surrounding words or expressions that may provide some extra pieces of information about the word in question and help you understand it.

You may be wondering why you should look at a word's context to determine its meaning. Well, sometimes, you may have to deal with polysemes, a word or expression with more than one meaning. Thanks to their multiple meanings, you cannot identify their correct meaning unless you consider the surrounding words or expressions.

For instance, consider this sentence: "He is my rock." What does *rock* mean in this sentence? Does it mean "a big stone"? The answer is no. Why? The context shows that *rock* is used to convey a different meaning in the sentence. It means "a pillar of strength or a support." This highlights the importance of context when dealing with polysemous words.

To improve your ability to use context clues to aid your reading and comprehension skills, you must be familiar with phrasal verbs, idiomatic expressions, and a host of other elements of grammar. Without them, you may always struggle to understand the context of a word or group of words.

Use the power of summary: Summary works similarly to annotating, but with a small difference. It requires you to summarize the main ideas of the material in your own words. This is an effective comprehension strategy because without making sense of the material, you cannot summarize it in your own words. So, your ability to provide an oral summary is indicative of your comprehension skills. The more effort you put into doing this, the better you become at reading and comprehension. Here are five tips that will boost your ability to summarize a study material:

Consider the length of your summary. A summary is not supposed to be as long as the paragraph or sentence since the goal is to draw out only the main ideas.

Identifying the main idea of a text is crucial to a good summary. Ask yourself what the author is trying to tell you. When you are done reading a document, the main idea(s) should stand out if you paid attention to your reading. You may likely find the main idea(s) at the beginning or end of a text. In contrast, some authors hide them somewhere within the material. Irrespective of where the main ideas are located, it is your responsibility to identify and isolate them for a proper summary.

Write the summary in your own words. This is possible only if you read and understood the material. If you do not, writing a good summary becomes nearly impossible. Thus, rather than recall it word for word, choose your own words to summarize the main ideas for your understanding. If you lift sentences or words verbatim from the material, your understanding of the material may be insufficient.

Endeavor to form a mental image of the material. What message is the material sending to you? Form a mental image of the message to boost your comprehension and recollection. This is possible only if you read and totally understood the material.

Use prior knowledge: Do you have background knowledge of the material? If you can relate to the content of a document, understanding it will be a lot easier.

So, during the preview stage, find out whether the material is familiar or not. If it is, take advantage of your prior knowledge to boost your understanding of the material. By building on what you already know, you can easily understand the areas you do not already know. This reduces the time it takes to go through the entire material and comprehend it.

This does not mean you have to know everything about the subject matter prior to reading the material. Your prior knowledge may be from hearing a related news story some time ago, a related story from a friend, something you saw in a movie, or something else that can give you background information about the subject. Once you start reading the material, such pieces of information will help your understanding.

Make inferences: Making inferences is your ability to read between the lines and identify unspoken or unwritten points. This skill requires you to use your previous knowledge to read between the lines or make a guess about something you are unfamiliar with. Considering the context may also be helpful. Since meanings may not be clearly stated in the material, explore all available avenues of what these could be.

It is important to note that the ability to make inferences from a study material does not come naturally. It is a skill you must develop over time. This skill requires you to have a solid grammatical understanding. You should be familiar with every element of grammar, not superficially, but ingrained enough that you will not struggle with the grammar section of the test. Without this knowledge, you may not figure out hidden meanings in a text.

Effective Reading Tips

Good readers do not only use the comprehension strategies listed above. They complement their efforts with the reading tips below.

These tips are classified into pre-reading tips, reading tips, and post-reading tips.

Pre-Reading Tips

Before you start reading a document, implement the following tips during the review stage and see the massive impact on your comprehension:

Outline your expectations. As the name suggests, this reading tip requires that you put your expectations down in writing as you skim through the material. Bring in the question strategy. Write down all the questions you want answers to. This prepares your mind for the reading task ahead.

While skimming the material, look at the preface and title page, if it has them. You may find some helpful information in these places. The table of contents is another part you should pay attention to. It is your roadmap as you embark on the reading or studying journey.

Some valuable pieces of information are sometimes hidden in the blurb on the back of a book. If the material has a blurb, take a look at this. Generally, check everywhere in the book when skimming, except the main content. When you are done with this, you can embark on the proper read-through.

Reading Tips

One of the most important reading tips is to identify your reading purpose. Why are you reading the material? Are you doing so as a form of entertainment or strictly for academic purposes? Identifying this purpose early on in the reading will help you beat distractions and focus on achieving your reading goals. Otherwise, you may be distracted and end up learning nothing tangible.

If you have a voluminous amount of study material, reading the entire material in one go may be daunting. The weight of the reading load may kill your interest in the material. If you plough on despite not wanting to, then you stand little chance of learning anything significant. Thus, a helpful tip is to break the study material into smaller and easier-to-read chunks. A chapter or two at a time may be all that you need to successfully read and understand it.

Note that there is no specific reading benchmark. Read at a convenient pace that will not wear you out and will make reading fun, thus increasing your comprehension ability.

Choose the best reading format. The proliferation of mobile devices and the internet has introduced many people to online reading. While this is laudable, not everyone is comfortable with reading on their device. Some still learn better from reading printed materials. Thus, determine whether you will print out the study material or read it online, based on the format you are more comfortable with. Your choice will greatly determine the extent of your comprehension.

Work on improving your vocabulary. As previously mentioned, limited vocabulary is the primary reason some people struggle with comprehension. If you identify this as your problem, you can fix the problem by working on your vocabulary.

The rule of thumb is to learn a new word daily. Do not let a day pass by without learning something new. For each word you learn, take a look at its related words such as synonyms, antonyms, and homophones. As you expand your vocabulary, your reading ability will improve drastically. That in turn will have a significant positive impact on your comprehension.

You may not naturally be inclined to pick up a dictionary and start learning new words. Only a handful of people can take that path. However, you have abundant resources that can help you learn new words. There are apps designed for this purpose and websites tailored to vocabulary that teach new words every day.

Some apps and other resources that can significantly help improve your vocabulary are Vocabulary.com, PowerVocab, 7 Little Words, Word to Word, A Word A Day Widget, and a host of others. Most of these are multiplatform resources that can be used by both Android and iOS users and are available for download from the Google Play Store and App Store, respectively.

Flash cards are other helpful resources. You can custom-make flash cards for learning purposes. Alternatively, if you do not have the time and material, purchase pre-made flash cards, such as 1100 Words You Need to Know. These flash cards contain some exercises that will help you learn not only individual words but idiomatic expressions too.

Learning new words will not have much impact on your vocabulary if you are content with just learning and memorizing them. For the best results, use these new words and idioms regularly. Seize every communication opportunity in which to apply them. The more you use such words, the better you become at their usage. The positive impact on your reading comprehension will be evident over time.

Set realistic reading goals. This is possible if you understand your reading strengths and weaknesses. Using this awareness, you can set realistic reading goals for yourself and stick to them. This enables you to read at your own pace without unnecessarily burdening yourself.

You will find this technique handy when reading difficult books or other materials that you cannot wrap your head around easily. Rather than read at a pace that makes comprehension difficult, go at your own pace and ensure you understand everything in each passage, no matter how long it takes you. Remember that you are not in a reading contest with anyone, but you are working on improving your comprehension ability. So, endeavor to read and understand each portion of a study document before moving to the next section or chapter. The knowledge of the current portion or chapter will serve as the foundation for the next.

If you are struggling with poor vocabulary, you can also start with materials that are below your vocabulary level. When you read a document you are comfortable with, you will not have much problem with comprehension. As your vocabulary improves, you can aim for more difficult materials. Take advantage of online quizzes that calculate your vocabulary and comprehension levels. This will help you determine the most appropriate materials to start with.

Take advantage of pleasure reading too. You can improve your comprehension when reading is fun. No matter your level, read entertainment materials, such as magazines and blog posts. As you devote more time to such materials, your interest in reading will improve considerably. Over time, you will overcome reading challenges and gradually improve your comprehension.

Get rid of distractions: The role distraction plays in limiting comprehension cannot be overemphasized. Without the ability to focus on your reading, you are at risk of not understanding the material. Thus, for improved comprehension, learn to eliminate all sources of distraction while reading.

Switch off your TV while reading. Set aside time to check your emails, chat with your friends online, and engage in other activities. Multitasking while reading will not work in your favor. You cannot divide your attention between several tasks and still comprehend whatever you are reading. Rather, a split attention will compound your comprehension issues. Limiting these activities to outside your study period will help you successfully overcome distractions and make the best use of your study time.

Your reading skills will be put into effect regularly as a police officer. You will not only be chasing criminals and suspects all over the city, you may also need to write reports, which will put your reading and writing skills to the test. If these are not deeply rooted, you may not be able to carry out your duties to the best of your ability.

Chapter Three: Grammar

The grammar section of the POST examination tests your knowledge of grammar. It will examine your proficiency in parts of speech, sentence construction, punctuation marks, and other elements of grammar. It will also test your ability to identify errors in sentences. Let us start with the building blocks of grammar: parts of speech.

Parts of Speech

Every sentence is built using some or all of the eight parts of speech. These are adjectives, adverbs, nouns, pronouns, interjections, conjunctions, verbs, and prepositions. A complete sentence must contain a verb and some or all of the other parts.

Adjectives

An adjective is a part of speech that is regularly used to qualify or provide more information about the noun in a sentence. Examples of adjectives abound. *Beautiful*, *tall*, *brilliant*, *exotic*, *black*, *young*, and *wealthy* are some common adjectives in daily use.

Without an adjective, you will not have much information about a specific noun. Adjectives usually precede the noun in the sentence, for instance in "We have a wealthy neighbor" and "The little girl is two years old." In these examples, the adjectives are *wealthy* and *little*. They provide some extra information about the *neighbor* and the *girl*, both nouns in the two sentences.

Adjectives are classified into several types. The common types of adjectives are possessive adjectives, number adjectives, interrogative adjectives, demonstrative adjectives, articles, attributive adjectives, and indefinite adjectives. Note that these different forms of adjectives are not used under the same conditions and are used for a wide range of purposes.

Possessive adjectives: Sometimes, adjectives are used to express ownership or possession when modifying a noun. Possessive adjectives are used for that purpose. In a similar vein to possessive pronouns, the possessive adjective is used to show that something belongs to a person, animal, or thing.

"Our house is behind the mall" and "His bicycle was stolen yesterday" are two examples of sentences that contain possessive adjectives. *Our* and *his* are the possessive adjectives in these sentences, respectively.

Number adjectives: A number adjective is the type of adjective used to give the numerical value of a thing or object. You can answer the question "How many?" with this adjective. Examples of number adjectives include the numbers 1 to infinity and their corresponding value in words. Thus, *8*, *eight*, *3*, *three*, and so on are all examples of number adjectives.

Interrogative adjectives: As indicated by the name, these adjectives are used for asking questions. The three interrogative adjectives are *which*, *what*, and *whose*. They are used for questions that ask what kind, which one, or whose is this.

Some examples are "Which book is yours?" and "What time should we expect you tomorrow?" These sentences contain the interrogative adjectives *which* and *what*, respectively.

Interrogative adjectives can also function as pronouns in a sentence. Thus, it is imperative to identify whether such an adjective is actually a pronoun or an adjective. An interrogative adjective precedes a noun in a sentence, unlike pronouns, which appear elsewhere.

Demonstrative adjectives: *This*, *these*, *that*, and *those* are examples of demonstrative adjectives. When they appear in a sentence, they indicate or demonstrate specific people or things. You can see some similarities between demonstrative adjectives and definite articles.

"Those boys are footballers" and "Give me that red helmet" are examples of demonstrative adjectives in use: *those* and *that*.

Articles: A special type of adjective specifically used to qualify non-specific things and people are articles. There are three articles: *a*, *the*, and *an*. The definite article *the* is used before a singular or plural noun. In the example "The boys walk slowly across the road," the article precedes the plural noun *boys* and singular noun *road*.

A and *an* are indefinite articles. The indefinite article *a* precedes a noun that starts with a consonant, while *an* comes before a noun that starts with a vowel. Examples are "An apple a day keeps the doctor away" and "A day is enough for the job."

Attributive adjectives: As the name implies, attributive adjectives are used to provide additional information about the attributes of a person or an object. They are used for describing an object's qualities, such as age, shape, color, and other features. *Real, best, beautiful, black, big*, and *tall* are typical examples of this type of adjective.

Note that an attributive adjective will usually precede a noun in a sentence. Two examples are "She is a beautiful girl" and "Kelvin is an intelligent actor," where *beautiful* and *intelligent* are examples of attributive adjectives.

Indefinite adjectives: Indefinite adjectives are specifically used to modify nouns that are non-specific objects or things. Since they are derived from indefinite pronouns, you can easily identify them in sentences. Some examples of this type of adjective are *any, many*, and *several*.

Consider these two examples: "There are several disgruntled elements in the workforce" and "Many people have lost hope in the system." Here, *several* and *many* modify the nouns *disgruntled elements* and *people*, respectively.

Adverbs

Adverbs are used to describe a verb, an adverb, or an adjective. They can also be used to modify or describe a sentence, group of words, clause, preposition, or determiner. Thus, to provide some additional information about the circumstance, manner, degree, time, and circumstance of an object, an adverb is used. They are also the part of speech used to express the level of certainty, frequency, and extent of the occurrence of an action. If the time of an action is very important, expect the adverb to start the sentence.

Adverbs are classified into five types. These are adverbs of time, adverbs of manner, adverbs of place, adverbs of degree, and adverbs of frequency.

Adverbs of time: To know when an action occurs, an adverb of time is used. Unlike adverbs of frequency that precede the main verb they qualify, adverbs of time may precede or succeed such verbs. The importance of the time of occurrence determines the adverb's position.

Some examples of adverbs of time are *yesterday, today, next year, annually, last year, often, occasionally, now, daily,* and so on. When any of these words appears in the place of an adverb in a sentence, it functions as an adverb of time.

Consider these sentences: "I went to my doctor's appointment yesterday" and "I'm planning to visit Paris next year." *Yesterday* and *next year* are the adverbs of time in the two sentences.

Adverbs of manner: The mannerism of the occurrence of an event is usually described with an adverb of manner. Once you see the adverb, you have a complete picture of the manner. Most examples of this adverb end in *-ly,* making them unarguably the most common adverbs. *Well* is another example of an adverb of manner.

Adverbs of manner are generally found immediately after intransitive verbs (verbs that do not need a direct object). For example, "The sector grew quickly after some new policies were introduced" and "She worked diligently for years before her breakthrough" contain the adverbs of manner *quickly* and *diligently.*

Adverbs of place: These adverbs help assign a place of occurrence to an event. This adverb comes immediately after the verb or the main object it qualifies. Sometimes, though, a sentence can be completed with an adverb of place. Some examples of this type of adverb are *outside, everywhere, below,* and *above.* If the adverb can answer the question "Where?"—it is an adverb of place.

Adverbs of degree: If the adverb can define the intensity level of an adverb, verb, or adjective, it is an adverb of degree. *Almost, enough,* and *quite* are some common examples of adverbs of degree. Adverbs of degree appear before whatever part of speech they modify.

"The food is extremely hot" contains the adverb of degree *extremely,* which modifies the adjective *hot.* The sentence "She was just sleeping when her phone rang" contains an adverb of degree, *just,* modifying a verb, *sleeping.* In a further example, "He was singing too beautifully," the adverb of degree is *too,* which modifies the adverb *beautifully.*

Adverbs of frequency: You can discern how frequently an event occurs through an adverb of frequency. These adverbs usually precede the main verb in the sentence and include examples such as *seldom*, *always*, *sometimes*, *again*, *regularly*, *normally*, *often*, and *rarely*.

Adverbs of frequency are usually placed between a sentence's subject and verb. For instance, "I always drive to work" has the adverb *always* between the subject *I* and the verb *drive*. However, with forms of the verb *to be*, the adverb of frequency is placed after the verb. This is shown in the following sentences: "He is never late to any appointment" and "Disappointments can be occasionally frustrating."

Nouns

The name by which a person, an object, or an animal is identified is a noun. *Chicago*, *Lawrence*, and *rainbow* are examples of nouns because they are used to identify a place, a person, and an object respectively. It is noteworthy that we can never run out of examples of nouns because we are surrounded by millions of them. From your house to the shirt you put on to your favorite pet, they are all examples of nouns.

Types of Nouns

The sheer number of nouns makes it necessary to classify them into different groups. The examples of nouns around you are classified into proper nouns, common nouns, abstract nouns, concrete nouns, possessive nouns, and collective nouns.

Proper Nouns

To identify single, specific entities from a group, a proper noun is used. Every individual member of a group of people, professionals, or things is a proper noun. For instance, when you mention a specific basketball player from a team, the referenced player is a proper noun. A doctor from a team of doctors is also a proper noun.

For instance, in the sentence "Mr. John, the security man, was here yesterday," *Mr. John* is a proper noun because it is a reference to a specific member of the security profession.

So, when you mention the specific name of an animal, a newspaper, a car, or idea, you are referencing a proper noun. Proper nouns are always capitalized.

Common Nouns

A common noun is the direct opposite of a proper noun. While a proper noun refers to a specific element of a group, a common noun is the group containing the proper nouns. Thus, *Federer* is a proper noun, but *tennis player* is a common noun. Pacific Ocean is a proper noun, but *ocean* is a common noun. Some other examples of common nouns are *teacher*, *writer*, *driver*, *cat*, *mountain*, and *building*.

It is noteworthy that common nouns are not usually capitalized, as you can see in the examples above. However, there are some exceptions to this rule. If a common noun appears in a title, it must be capitalized. The same rule applies if this type of noun begins a sentence.

Abstract Nouns

A type of noun that refers to invisible concepts is an abstract noun. Every member of this noun group is a concept or idea that can be only felt or experienced but not physically seen.

Abstract nouns are used to express events, social concepts, qualities, concepts, and other related ideas. Thus, when you experience or display your knowledge, anger, intelligence, love, liberty, charity, anger, democracy, freedom, or generosity, you are either experiencing or displaying a form of abstract noun.

"The little boy's bravery astounded the onlookers" and "Her intelligence has won her international recognitions" are two examples of abstract nouns in sentences. Note that both *bravery* and *intelligence* are invisible but can be expressed or felt.

Concrete Nouns

In sharp contrast to an abstract noun is a concrete noun. In this context, *abstract* and *concrete* are antonyms. Thus, while you cannot see but can only feel the former, the latter refers to something you can feel and touch. Every solid object around you is a concrete noun. The chair you sit on while reading this text, your mobile device on which you are reading it, your glasses, your apartment, and other objects are all concrete nouns provided they are visible and can be touched. Both common and proper nouns can also be concrete nouns.

Concrete nouns are classified into countable and uncountable. The former refers to the class of concrete nouns that can be individually counted. As such, they can be pluralized. Examples include *chair*, *book*, *house*, and so on. In the latter group are nouns that can be neither counted nor pluralized. *Water*, *sugar*, and *rice* fall into this group. Nobody can count rice or salt (only grains of rice or salt). Water is completely uncountable.

Possessive Nouns

Possession or ownership can be best described with possessive nouns. A possessive noun will be immediately followed by an apostrophe and an *s* to show the possession. This rule applies to singular nouns. For plural nouns, an *s* will not be added after the apostrophe because a plural noun already comes with an *s*.

Consider these examples: "This is Kenny's dog" and "The boys' mothers are successful businesswomen." The former illustrates a singular possessive noun, *Kenny's*, while the latter illustrates a plural possessive noun, *boys'*. Take note of the apostrophe placement in both sentences for clearer understanding.

Collective Nouns

You can identify a collection of items with a collective noun. *Flock*, *crowd*, *committee*, *team*, *band*, *army*, and *choir* are examples of collective nouns you may regularly come across.

Thus, expressions such as *a galaxy of stars*, *a bouquet of flowers*, and *a crowd of people* all contain collective nouns. Other examples are *a flock of sheep*, *a litter of puppies*, *a pack of hounds*, *a school of fish*, and *an army of ants*.

Pronouns

When looking for an alternative to nouns in sentences, pronouns are used. They perform the same function as a noun in whatever sentence they appear. The types of pronouns are possessive pronouns, personal pronouns, reflexive pronouns, intensive pronouns, relative pronouns, interrogative pronouns, indefinite pronouns, and demonstrative pronouns.

Possessive Pronouns

Just like its noun counterpart, a possessive pronoun is the type of pronoun specifically used for showing possession or ownership. Thus, rather than use a possessive noun, you can use a possessive pronoun to achieve the same result. *Mine*, *hers*, *his*, *ours*, and *theirs* are some pronouns that fall into the possessive class.

"The canteen was all theirs" and "The showroom around the corner is his" are examples of how possessive pronouns are used in sentences. Possessive pronouns are used extensively in sentences to avoid needless repetition.

Personal Pronouns

Personal pronouns are pronouns that are used to replace people's names. As a result of their ability to replace a personal noun, this type of pronoun can serve as the subject or object of a sentence. There are two types of personal pronoun. These are objective and subjective personal pronouns.

As the names suggest, objective pronouns can serve as the object of the sentence, while subjective pronouns can be the subject of the sentence. *It*, *she*, *you*, and *we* are some subjective personal pronouns, while objective pronouns include *him*, *her*, *them*, and *us*.

Reflexive Pronouns

A reflexive pronoun is a pronoun that comes after an adjective, adverb, or noun. The word the reflexive pronoun refers to must exist in the same clause with the pronoun. *Itself*, *yourselves*, *ourselves*, and *themselves* are members of the reflexive pronoun group. Most reflexive pronouns end with the suffixes -self or -*selves*.

Here are some examples: "Because I was so tired to cook myself, I ordered takeout." "The boys are too young to go home themselves."

Intensive Pronouns

Intensive pronouns are used to intensify or emphasize nouns and pronouns. Intensive pronouns are easily recognized by their *-self* or *-selves* suffix. They come immediately after the pronoun or noun they emphasize. Thus, when you come across some pronouns, such as *myself, herself, themselves,* or *yourself,* they are intensive pronouns.

Relative Pronouns

Relative pronouns perform some special functions in a sentence. They are specifically the connector between a clause or a phrase and a noun or a pronoun to provide the reader with some additional information about the part of speech they are modifying. Relative pronouns include *whichever, who, whoever, whomever, whose, which, when,* and *that.*

Relative pronouns can stand alone as either the subject or the object of a sentence. "Whoever comes first in the test gets a scholarship" and "Give the book to whomever you meet at home" show how a relative pronoun can serve either of the two purposes.

Interrogative Pronouns

Who, which, whose, and *what* are common examples of interrogative pronouns. As you can see from the examples, these pronouns are used for asking questions. No wonder they are otherwise known as the *wh-* words. Interrogative pronouns are great for asking both indirect and direct questions.

Indefinite Pronouns

You can make an indirect reference to a noun with an indefinite pronoun such as *everyone, everything, anything, someone, none, little, much, either, another, neither, each, nobody,* or any of the other members of the indefinite pronoun group. They are referred to as indefinite pronouns because they do not reference a particular person or object.

Some indefinite pronouns end in *-one* and *-body* (e.g., *everyone, everybody*). Such pronouns are most often singular.

Demonstrative Pronouns

Demonstrative pronouns are derived from demonstrative words. These are words that are used to refer to a specific entity, unlike indefinite pronouns. Some demonstrative pronouns are *this, that, those,* and *these.*

Ordinal numbers can also perform the role of demonstrative adjectives in sentences. These are numbers such as *fifth, first, tenth,* and so on. For instance, *fourth* is a demonstrative adjective in the sentence "Wednesday is the fourth day of the week."

Interjections

Strong feelings and emotions are expressed with this part of speech. Otherwise known as exclamations, they are used to express happiness, hunger, love, disgust, and an array of other emotional feelings. "Oh my God!" "Oh dear," and "Hurrah!" are some examples of how to express emotional feelings with interjections. As shown in two of the examples, many interjections have an exclamation point (!).

Conjunctions

Two or more words can be connected with a conjunction. It can also be used to join multiple clauses or phrases. The types of conjunction are adverbial conjunctions, subordinating conjunctions, coordinating conjunctions, and correlative conjunctions.

Adverbial Conjunctions

Another name for an adverbial conjunction is a conjunctive adverb. These conjunctions come in handy when connecting two or more independent clauses (clauses with their own subject and verb that can stand on their own). When an adverbial conjunction appears in a sentence, it is usually preceded by a semicolon and succeeded with a comma.

Examples of adverbial conjunctions are *meanwhile, in contrast, accordingly, finally, however, therefore, on the other hand, consequently, nevertheless, likewise, besides,* and *finally.*

Subordinating Conjunctions

If two clauses do not share the same grammatical value, they are usually connected with a subordinating conjunction. These come in handy when connecting a dependent clause with an independent clause.

Unless, *since*, *whether*, *until*, *although*, and *because* are some examples of subordinating conjunctions. For instance, "He was working although he was hungry" shows how the subordinating conjunction, *although* is used to join the independent clause *He was working* with the dependent clause *although he was hungry*.

Coordinating Conjunctions

A clear distinction between a subordinating conjunction and a coordinating conjunction is that while the former is used for connecting clauses of different grammatical values, the latter is used for connecting clauses of equal grammatical value, such as two independent clauses or two dependent clauses. Note some examples:

"The boy enjoys watching football, but he hates playing soccer games" is an example of two independent clauses joined by a comma and *but*. "You can eat your breakfast with a fork or spoon" is an example of two grammatically equal phrases, *fork* and *spoon*, joined by *or*.

Correlative Conjunctions

The relationship between two or more words or ideas can be expressed with a correlative conjunction. This type of conjunction comes in pairs and is used to show the contrast between words or ideas.

For instance, in the sentence "The little girl is both silly and clever," the correlative conjunction *both/and* shows how the subject *the little girl* has both those traits in equal measure.

<u>Verbs</u>

As an important part of speech, a verb is used to define the subject's action in a sentence. Without a verb, you will be lost, with zero idea about what action the subject performs.

Verbs occur in different forms. These are regular verbs, linking verbs, irregular verbs, finite verbs, infinite verbs, and intransitive verbs. Let us consider them now.

Regular Verbs

A regular verb is a type of verb that forms its past tense and past participle form by simply adding *d* or *ed* to the verb. Regular verbs abound and include *clean*, *walk*, *talk*, *dance*, *play*, *accept*, and countless others.

Linking Verbs

A verb can be used to connect a subject to an adjective or a noun in a sentence's predicate. Such a verb is referred to as a linking verb. The list of linking verbs include *look*, *grow*, *appear*, *sound*, and more. Consider some examples:

"After burning the midnight oil, he looked exhausted." "Bola acted nervous when she encountered the celebrity." In the first sentence, the subject is the pronoun *he*, while the adjective is *exhausted*. The verb *looked* connects the two. In the second sentence, the verb *acted* connects the subject *Bola* and the adjective *nervous*.

Irregular Verbs

Irregular verbs are the direct opposite of regular verbs. While regular verbs follow the addition of *d* or *ed* to form their past and past participle forms, irregular verbs do not follow a regular pattern.

For instance, the past tense of *break* is *broke*, while the past participle is *broken*. In the same vein, the past tense of *drink* is *drank*, and *drunk* is the past participle. On the other hand, the irregular verb *bid* has the same past and past participle forms. The same pattern applies to *shut*.

Finite Verbs

Finite verbs are not a type of verb, but rather a form of verb that is dependent on the subject. Thus, they are used to define the subject of a sentence and the time of the action performed by the subject.

For instance, *eat*, *dance*, *walk*, and *sleep* are examples of finite verbs, whose tense and form can provide information about the time of an action and the subject, respectively. "He eats vegetables" and "I will eat" are two different uses of the same verb, *eat*. In the first sentence, *eat* defines what the subject does, whereas in the second sentence, it defines what the subject will do in the future.

Nonfinite Verbs

A verb that is preceded with *to* is referred to as a nonfinite verb. When such a verb is used, it does not give the tense of the action. For instance, "To succeed in life, you must be ready to overcome some challenges." In this sentence, the verb *succeed* is preceded by *to*. We say this verb is in its infinitive form.

Intransitive Verbs

An intransitive verb is a verb that does not take a direct object. Thus, you cannot easily identify the recipient of the verb's action in the sentence. "He was living the life of his dreams" is an example of the intransitive verb *live* in action. "He has been sleeping since his arrival from work" and "The toddler slept peacefully after a shower" are two other examples using the intransitive verb *sleep*.

Transitive Verbs

Unlike an intransitive verb that does not need a direct object, a transitive verb takes a direct object. This enables readers to identify the recipient of the verb's action in a sentence. Take the sentence "He kicked a ball on his way home from school." The transitive verb is *kicked*. This verb takes the direct object *ball*, which is the recipient of the action performed by the verb.

Prepositions

A preposition is a part of speech that connects nouns, pronouns, and phrases in a sentence. Prepositions can be used to connect people, objects, and other relevant pieces of information. They precede nouns and prefix gerund verbs under certain conditions.

Prepositions are classified into prepositions for time, prepositions for instrument, prepositions for place, prepositions for agent, and prepositions for direction.

Prepositions for Time

A preposition for time defines the specific time of occurrence of an event. This may refer to an occurrence in the past, present, or future. The preposition may also refer to a time of the day, a day of the week, a year of the month, and other related information.

These two examples demonstrate prepositions for time: "We left the seminar at exactly 4 p.m." "Christmas is always on the 25th of December." In the first example, *at* is the preposition and is followed by the hour. In the second, *on* is the preposition and is followed by the day and month. So, both examples give the specific time of an event.

Prepositions for Instrument

Devices, machines, and instruments are defined by prepositions for instrument. The following are prepositions for instrument: *by, with the help of,* and *with*. It is noteworthy that this preposition is preceded by a noun, not a verb. "She goes to work by car" and "She loosened the screw with a screwdriver" are two examples of how a preposition for instrument is used. *By* is the preposition in the first sentence, with the machine being *car*, while *with* is the preposition in the second sentence with the instrument being *screwdriver*.

Prepositions for Place

A class of preposition specifically for addresses, places, or locations is a preposition for place. The most commonly used prepositions for place are *in*, *on*, and *at*.

These prepositions are used under different conditions. When mentioning an object's surface, *on* is used. For example: "The book is on the shelf." For defining a physical or virtual boundary, *in* is the ideal preposition. When making reference to specific places, you can use *at*.

Prepositions for Agent

Prepositions for agent express the relationship between the subject of a sentence and the accompanying verb or action. *By* and *with* are examples of prepositions for agent.

"The play was written by the legendary William Shakespeare" and "We will visit the remote villages by road" demonstrate how prepositions for agent can express the relationship between a subject and a verb.

Prepositions for Direction

Prepositions for direction are used to furnish readers with more information about the subject or verb of a sentence. Here are some examples of this preposition: *to*, *into*, *through*, and *toward*.

"The little boy is crawling toward the TV" and "She ran through the crowds" are two examples of prepositions for direction at work. In the first sentence, *toward* gives the direction the boy is crawling in. In the second, *through* gives more information on where she is running with regard to the crowds.

Punctuation Marks

Punctuation marks are a set of marks such as commas, periods, question marks, and a host of others that are used for dividing a piece of writing into clauses and sentences. There are 14 punctuation marks. These marks and their uses are discussed below.

Question Marks (?)

A question mark indicates an interrogative sentence. Any interrogative sentence must end with a question mark to differentiate it from a declarative sentence that ends with a full stop or period.

"What are you doing at the moment?" and "What is the essence of the new policy?" are two interrogative sentences as shown by their question marks.

Quotation Marks (" ")

Just as the name implies, quotation marks are used for making quotations. This is especially useful when giving a direct quote from a person, a book, or any other source. For instance, Smith wrote, "the fire ignited from the high temperatures and highly combustible materials present." The words inside the quotation marks are reported exactly as written by the author.

Quotation marks are also known as speech marks and can be used to convey speech. Consider this example: "I will attend to the dishes as soon as I am done with the assignment," the boy told his mother. Here, the words inside the quotation marks are reported exactly as spoken by the boy.

Parentheses (())

A pair of parentheses can provide additional information about a sentence. Note that without the additional information, the sentence will still convey a complete thought. For instance, "The couple (who just moved into the neighborhood) are away on vacation." The phrase *who just moved into the neighborhood* is enclosed in parentheses to furnish the reader with more information about the couple in question. A pair of commas can perform the same function: "The couple, who just moved into the neighborhood, are away on vacation."

Hyphens (-)

A hyphen is a punctuation mark that connects two or more words to form a compound term. Examples of such compound terms include *well-known*, *full-time*, and *well-behaved*, among others.

Brackets ([])

Brackets are used for clarification or technical explanation of the words or expressions used. If you remove the explanation in the brackets, the sentence will still retain its original meaning. Consider this example: They [Mr. and Mrs. Ken] are members of Silicon Valley. As you can see, while the information in the brackets help us to understand who *they* are, you can remove it without affecting the sentence.

Commas (,)

If two elements or ideas are expressed in a sentence, a comma is used to distinguish between the elements or ideas. They are also used in writing dates or separating numbers.

Consider this example: "The girl is tall, bold, and beautiful." Commas have been used here to separate elements in a list. Consider the sentence "The boy is not only brilliant, he is handsome too." Here, the comma separates two elements of being brilliant and also being handsome.

Braces ({})

Braces are curly notations that are used to show that a list of items or lines of texts is a single entity and should be treated as such. Although braces are not commonly used in everyday writing, this punctuation mark is extensively used in programming. Braces are also sometimes used when writing mathematical expressions.

Apostrophes (')

An apostrophe may serve either of two purposes in a sentence. It may show a contraction, indicating the removal of a letter from a word. For instance, *isn't* is a contraction of *is not*. *He's* and *let's* are contracted forms of *he is/ he has* and *let us*, respectively.

It can also be used to show possession. For example, "This is Ade's book" and "Here are the boy's parents" show that the book belongs to Ade and the parents belong to the boy. In either case, possession or ownership is defined by an apostrophe.

Ellipsis (…)

Three periods (…) are commonly used to represent this punctuation mark. Sometimes, it is represented by three asterisks (***). In printing or writing, an ellipsis is used to show omission of words or letters. For example: "The boy started counting the book from one, two, three … twenty." So, the unnecessary words between three and twenty have been omitted with the ellipsis. Based on the context, the reader can easily guess the omitted words.

When ellipses are used within quotations, it is specifically to move from one phrase to another while unnecessary words are omitted in the process. For instance: The fundamental Human rights include "the right to worship … as enshrined in the constitution." Here, some words have been omitted, but the meaning remains intact.

Dashes (– —)

A dash is a punctuation mark that is used for separating groups of words. There are two types of dash: the en dash and em dash. Some people mistake the en dash for a hyphen. However, it is twice the length of a hyphen. This punctuation mark is used in the printing industry or in writing to indicate connections or a range. It can also be used for differentiations. For instance, "World War 1 was fought from 1914–1918."

The em dash is longer than its en counterpart. It can perfectly replace a parenthesis, comma, or colon for improved readability. For instance: "She gave him the right answer—a resounding *yes*."

Colons (:)

A colon can be used for three purposes in sentences. First, it is used after an independent clause that introduces an example, an explanation, or a series. For example, "The boy can play several musical instruments: piano, drums, guitar, and trumpet."

Second, a colon can separate two independent clauses when the second clause sheds more light on the first. In this capacity, it performs a similar function to a semicolon. For instance, "I couldn't make it to the party: I was pretty busy."

Less commonly, the colon is used to show emphasis. Consider this example: "Although she suffers from a terminal illness, she has a source of hope: her mother." In this sentence, the colon emphasizes from where the subject derives her hope.

Semicolons (;)

This punctuation mark connects independent clauses. It replaces a period when the relationship between the two clauses is more pronounced. For instance, consider these two sentences: "Jane was hurt." "Her boyfriend intentionally hurt her." You can merge the two sentences into one with a semicolon, thus: "Jane was hurt; her boyfriend intentionally hurt her."

Period/Full Stop (.)

A full stop is otherwise known as a period. It is unarguably the most frequently used punctuation mark. It is used at the end of an abbreviation or a complete/declarative sentence. As you can see, each sentence in this paragraph contains a period to mark its end.

More so, the following sentences show how a full stop is used in abbreviations: "Today is St. Peter's Day." "The World Health Organization (W.H.O.) is at the forefront of the fight against the deadly disease."

It is vital to use the correct punctuation marks when writing sentences. You cannot imagine writing an interrogative sentence without the mandatory question mark. Such a sentence is grammatically flawed.

Punctuation Errors

Punctuation marks are great because they make your writing easy to read and digest. On the other hand, a piece of writing with tons of punctuation errors will be difficult to understand. Your audience may not be comfortable with such a piece either. Some common punctuation errors are listed below, along with advice on how to avoid them.

Missing commas: While some people make the mistake of using too many commas in inappropriate places, some avoid using them altogether. This may generate some grammatical errors in addition to increasing the reading difficulty. Consider this example: "I went home yesterday and I didn't meet anyone at home and so I went to my granny's." This is undoubtedly a difficult sentence to read. However, if commas are used appropriately, the sentence will not only be easy to read, but meaningful too.

Excess exclamation marks: This is gradually becoming a norm among social media users. It is not uncommon for people to use multiple exclamation marks for a single sentence. This error should be avoided at all costs. No matter your degree of excitement or disappointment, do not use more than a single exclamation mark.

Excess exclamation marks, aside from being grammatically wrong, are a distraction to readers. Readers may be at a loss at the rationale behind this excess.

Dash vs. hyphen: Another punctuation mark error is mixing up the dash and the hyphen. While they are seemingly identical, the en dash and em dash are both longer than a hyphen and used for different purposes. Hyphens are used for making compound words, such as *one-week*, *well-known*, and *time-based*. On the other hand, the longer em dash is used to indicate a change in thought or idea.

Colon vs. semicolon: This punctuation error arises from the fact that the colon and semicolon are often used interchangeably by people who do not understand the difference between them. So, they may end up using a semicolon where a colon is appropriate, and vice versa. This is an example: "He loves three subjects; math, English, and literature." The semicolon in that sentence is not suitable since the list is not an independent clause. The appropriate punctuation mark is a colon.

If you are confused about the two, remember that a colon precedes a set of items, while a semicolon is the ideal punctuation mark for separating two distinct thoughts that may be related in some way. Alternatively, you can replace a semicolon with a period and break the sentence into two.

Unnecessary quotation marks: As previously mentioned, quotation marks are designed for making direct quotes. Sadly, some use these marks sporadically, irrespective of whether they are making direct quotations or not. While writing reports or any other form of writing, resist the desire to use quotation marks as you please.

Unnecessary apostrophes: The function of an apostrophe in a sentence has been defined in the previous section. However, a common error is using an apostrophe where it does not naturally belong. Consider this example: "The boy's are coming." In this phrase, the apostrophe has no place, as *boys* is a plural noun, not a possessive noun. Thus, for a correct sentence, it should be removed.

Too many commas: Some people use too many commas in a sentence. Those who use this punctuation mark randomly have little or zero knowledge of its usage. Hence, to avoid this error, learn where and how to use commas and apply the knowledge while writing. Consider this: "On getting to the rendezvous, I didn't see him, so, I went to the nearby mall, got some stuff, and went home." This is a typical example of too many commas in a sentence.

Although there is no stipulated number of commas acceptable for a sentence, you can do better by breaking the sentence into two or more sentences to reduce the number of commas and make it more readable. Here is a better rendering: "On getting to the rendezvous, I didn't see him. I went to the nearby mall, got some stuff, and went home." While the number of commas in each sentence has been reduced, the message remains unchanged.

Quotation mark placement: Many people struggle with punctuation in a quoted sentence. One confusing aspect is whether the punctuation mark concluding the quote should be outside or inside the quotation mark. If the punctuation mark is naturally a part of the quoted sentence, it should be placed with the sentence inside the quotation mark.

Consider these two examples: "When are we visiting the countryside"? and "When are we visiting the countryside?" The former sentence is grammatically inaccurate, while the latter is correct. This is because the question mark belongs with the quoted question and should therefore be inside the quotation marks. So, when making quotations, avoid committing this punctuation blunder.

The Oxford comma: The Oxford comma punctuation error arises as a result of the lack of a consistent rule guiding the use of the last comma (the Oxford comma) when making a list. One school of thought believes that the last comma should be used before the final item in a list, whereas another school of thought believes it should be skipped. Currently, there is an ongoing debate about which convention is right and which is wrong. In the absence of a consensus, use either of the two formats. The key is consistency. Do not jump from one format to another within the same text.

These are two examples to demonstrate the two styles: "The bag contains two yellow balls, a handkerchief, a mirror, and some writing materials." "The bag contains two yellow balls, a handkerchief, a mirror and some writing materials." Notice that the comma between *mirror* and *and* has been skipped in the second sentence, while the Oxford comma is included in the first sentence. Both expressions are correct.

Sentences

A sentence is a group of words combined to convey a meaning. It is the basic unit of the English language.

Types of Sentence

There are different types of sentence in English. These are declarative sentences, imperative sentences, interrogative sentences, and exclamative sentences. The classification is based on the function of each sentence. Here is a description of each sentence type:

Declarative Sentences

A declarative statement is simply referred to as a statement. This sentence provides the reader with a piece of information. It is a simple statement that contains a subject, a verb, and other elements. Declarative sentences are either negative or positive.

For instance, some positive declarative sentences are "I will come tomorrow" and "I love having rice and stew for breakfast." On the other hand, "I don't like swimming" and "We didn't leave home last Sunday" are examples of negative declarative statements.

Imperative Sentences

Imperative sentences are sentences that give commands. They are used to tell people to do something or take an action. Like the other sentences mentioned above, imperative sentences can be positive or negative. They end with either an exclamation mark or a period. Take a look at some examples: "Give her a cup of coffee." "Wait until his arrival." These two are positive imperative sentences.

In contrast, "Don't go until he gets here" and "Don't open the package without proper authorization" are two examples of negative imperative sentences.

Interrogative Sentences

As the name implies, interrogative sentences ask questions. They are the type of sentences used to request information. No wonder they are incomplete without a question mark. They can also be positive or negative. Consider some examples:

"What are you doing at the moment?" and "When is the POST examination coming up?" These are two examples of positive interrogative sentences.

Conversely, "Why didn't you go for the interview?" and "Who wasn't present at the pass out parade?" are examples of negative interrogative sentences.

Exclamative Sentences

This type of sentence is commonly referred to as exclamation. As previously mentioned, these are the sentences that are used for expressing strong surprise or emotions. Naturally, exclamative sentences end with an exclamation mark.

"What exciting news!" "What a liar!" "This is extraordinary!" These are a few examples of exclamative sentences.

Sentence Structure

Sentence structure refers to the arrangement of the components of a sentence such as words, clauses, and phrases. A sentence's meaning may be dependent on its structure. There are four grammatical structures. These are simple sentences, complex sentences, compound sentences, and compound-complex sentences.

Simple Sentences

A sentence is said to be simple if it consists of one independent clause. This is a type of clause that can stand on its own and make a complete sentence. Some examples include: "She is coming." "He throws the ball." "Today is Monday."

Compound Sentences

Unlike a simple sentence, a compound sentence contains at least two independent clauses. These clauses are connected by a semicolon or a conjunction. Thus, each member of a compound sentence can form an independent and complete sentence on its own.

Some examples of compound sentences are "I love soccer, but she loves cricket." "We can fix it, but we have to do it properly." "She is a student, and he is a businessman." Each of these sentences is a compound sentence containing two independent clauses joined by *but* and *and*. Some other coordinating conjunctions used for connecting such clauses are *or*, *yet*, *for*, *nor*, and *so*.

Complex Sentences

A complex sentence consists of two clauses of different grammatical values. While one of the clauses is an independent clause, the other is a dependent clause.

A dependent clause begins with either a relative pronoun or a subordinating conjunction. It contains a verb and a subject. Nevertheless, it cannot stand on its own and convey a complete and meaningful thought.

Some examples of complex sentences are "We arrived at our destination late because we had a flat tire." "Jane and Harry left home in a hurry after they got a phone call from their friend." In each example, the first part of the sentence is an independent clause while the second part is a dependent clause. The clauses can be switched around as long as a comma is added: "After they got a phone call from their friend, Jane and Harry left home in a hurry."

Some subordinating conjunctions that can begin a dependent clause are *because, whether, after, though, although, before, while, till, since,* and *how.* Others are *that, when, until, if, than,* and *once.* Likewise, the following relative pronouns can also begin a dependent clause: *which, whose, that, whom,* and *who.*

Compound-Complex Sentences

A compound-complex sentence consists of both types of clauses: independent and dependent. However, for a sentence to be considered compound-complex, it must consist of at least a dependent clause and a minimum of two independent clauses.

It is imperative to make it clear that there is a distinction between types of sentence and types of sentence structure. Knowing the difference between the two will improve your knowledge of grammar considerably.

Complete and Incomplete Sentences

A sentence can be either complete or incomplete. A sentence is considered complete if it has these three elements: a subject, an object, and a verb. The subject of a sentence is either a noun or a pronoun. Next comes the verb in the sentence: the action performed by the subject. Of course, the verb will attract an object, the recipient of the action.

For instance, in the example "She reads her literature book every day," the pronoun *she* is the subject of the sentence. The verb is *reads*. The recipient of the reading action is her *literature book*.

Consider another example: "Tony kicked the ball over the fence." The subject of the sentence is *Tony*. The sentence centers on him. Next is the action word or verb, *kicked*. What did he kick? The ball. Hence, *the ball* is the object of the sentence because it accepts the kicking action performed by the subject.

In addition to containing these three elements, a complete sentence must also convey a complete and meaningful thought. Thus, if a sentence contains a subject, a verb, and an object and does not convey a meaningful thought, it is incomplete. A sentence that lacks any of the elements is considered a sentence fragment.

The rule of thumb is that a complete sentence must start with an upper case, or capital, letter. A form of punctuation such as an exclamation mark, a question mark, or a full stop must signify the end of the sentence. Without such a punctuation mark, it is difficult to ascertain that the sentence has been completed.

Common Sentence Construction Errors

Proper sentence construction is crucial to writing a complete sentence. However, many people are prone to committing sentence construction errors that stand between them and their reader. When a sentence is not properly constructed or contains the errors highlighted below, the writer will fail to convey the right meaning to their audience.

There are three common sentence construction errors. These are run-on sentences, sentence fragments, and comma splices. If you can identify these errors while writing, you can avoid them and spare your audience the disappointment associated with their inability to make sense of your message. Let us consider these common errors and cover practical ways you can avoid them.

Sentence Fragments

Sentence fragments are incomplete sentences. Most fragments have at least one of the sentence construction elements, especially a subject. However, they do not have a verb or a predicate (a part that informs us about the subject). The incompleteness of such a sentence means it cannot convey a complete and meaningful thought.

Consider this example: "She beautiful." This sentence contains a subject, *she* and an adjective, *beautiful*. Thus, it contains just one of the three elements of a complete sentence. In view of that, it is an incomplete sentence or a sentence fragment.

Comma Splices

Comma splices are a sentence construction error that commonly occurs when two independent clauses are joined together with a comma. Joining two independent clauses with a comma is not grammatically correct, and a sentence with such an error blurs the real message the author is trying to convey.

Comma splices increase the reading difficulty of a piece of writing, as they interrupt the flow. Let us consider some ways you can fix the comma splice error.

You can avoid comma splices if you cultivate the habit of using appropriate punctuation marks. A semicolon can join two independent clauses. So, if you are incorrectly using a comma, simply replace it with a semicolon to fix the problem.

You may also want to consider splitting the sentence into two, especially if the two independent clauses are not particularly related to one another. When two independent clauses are joined, you can separate these into two independent sentences. For instance, consider the incorrect sentence "Tony can't go to work, he is sick." When broken into two sentences, you have "Tony can't go to work" and "He is sick." Always remember that this solution applies to two independent clauses only, not to an independent and a dependent clause.

Another effective solution is to use a coordinating conjunction after the comma. Thus, "Tony can't go to work, he is sick" becomes "Tony can't go to work, for he is sick." The introduction of *for*, a coordinating conjunction, removes the error. Alternatively, you could use a subordinating conjunction to make one clause dependent. When you use *because*, the sentence turns into "Tony can't go to work because he is sick."

Run-On Sentences

This error occurs when two independent clauses are merged to form a single sentence. The complex sentence resulting from the merger lacks the punctuation needed to make a correct sentence.

"We are going home we are done for today" is an example of a run-on sentence. The appropriate punctuation marks needed to make the complex sentence both complete and meaningful are lacking.

To fix a run-on error, adopt any of the solutions recommended for fixing comma splices.

Linguistics

Linguistics simply means the study of language. Through its many branches, such as phonology, semantics, syntax, and morphology, speakers are better able to understand a language. The roles played by each of these branches are outlined below with a discussion on how these can improve your knowledge of the English language:

Semantics

Semantics is a branch of linguistics that deals with the meaning and interpretation of words, symbols, and sentence structure. It focuses on boosting a reader's comprehension ability by helping them understand both the literal and figurative meanings of a specific word. Semantics is divided into connotative semantics and denotative semantics.

Denotation is the literal meaning of a word. This is usually found in a dictionary.

The connotation focuses on the implied or figurative meaning of a word. This is beyond its direct meaning in the dictionary.

Thus, you should understand that words can have both literal and figurative meanings. Through studying connotations, you will understand whether the figurative or literal meaning of a word is implied in a sentence. The same word may have different meanings in a paragraph if one sentence uses it denotatively and another one focuses on its connotative meaning.

Here are some words and their denotative and connotative meanings:

"The lady is hot." Is the lady running a high temperature or extremely attractive? The former is its denotative meaning, while the latter is its connotative meaning. You can count on the context to give you a clue about the meaning of a specific word. This applies to every word that can have more than one meaning in a sentence.

Morphology

Morphology is another branch of linguistics. It is the study of word formation, the relationship between words, and word structure (such as root words, suffixes, and prefixes). Having this background information aids your understanding of a specific word.

For instance, a prefix is a word or group of letters added to the beginning of another word to make a new word with a meaning distinct from the original. Some common examples of prefixes and their meanings are *im*, meaning "not." When *im* is added to *possible*, the new word *impossible* is formed. *Pre* means "before." The meaning is pronounced in words such as *preview*, *pre-natal*, and *preconceived*, among others.

While prefixes are added at the beginning of words to give them new meanings, suffixes are added to the end of a root word to form a new word with a new meaning. *Age* is a suffix that indicates a state or condition. Examples are *vintage*, *marriage*, *leakage*, *breakage*, and a host of others. Adding the *er* suffix in the same manner denotes the doer of an action. A driver is someone who drives, a teacher teaches, and a painter paints.

Learn to spot key root words, prefixes, and suffixes when discerning the meaning of a word.

Concord

Concord refers to the agreement between the subject and the verb in a sentence. For a complete and error-free sentence, the two components of that sentence must be in agreement.

Some rules establish the relationship between the two. These rules are generally referred to as the rule of concord. Here are the 22 rules that determine this agreement:

Rule 1

If the subject is singular, the verb must be singular too.

This rule is pretty simple. It implies that singular subjects attract singular verbs too. But what constitutes singular subjects and verbs?

A singular subject is a noun or pronoun that refers to a single person or thing. Such a subject does not end with an *s* as do plural subjects. Some examples of singular subjects include *table*, *chair*, *car*, and the name of a single person, animal, place, or thing.

On the other hand, most singular verbs in the present tense end with an *s*. common examples of singular verbs include *goes*, *comes*, *dances*, *eats*, *reads*, and more. Thus, when you use a singular subject, the corresponding verb should be singular too.

Here are some examples of singular subjects and singular verbs:

"The boy loves dancing." The subject of the sentence is *the boy*. As you can see, the reference is made to a single boy. Hence, it must attract a singular verb: a verb with an *s*. Therefore *loves* is used as the verb, not *love*. Some other examples are: "Tolu lives in that neighborhood" and "Kenny sings like a pro."

Rule 2

If the subject is plural, the verb should be plural too.

This is another straightforward rule. Here, a plural subject refers to more than a single person or object. This implies that the sentence focuses on more than one person or thing. Plural subjects usually have an *s* at the end. Some examples of plural subjects are *boys*, *girls*, *the boy and his mother*, and *the birds*.

Plural verbs, unlike their singular counterparts, do not end with an *s*. They are used together with plural subjects. Some examples of plural verbs are *go*, *come*, *read*, *sing*, and *walk*. Let us use the examples above to show the difference between the two rules.

"The boy and his brother love dancing." The subject has been changed from *the boy*, a single person, to *the boy and his brother*, two people. Hence, the subject is now plural. Thus, according to the rule, the verb must also change to reflect the change in the subject. Hence, it changes from *loves* to *love*.

"Tolu lives in that neighborhood" may changes to "Tolu and her friend live in that neighborhood," while "Kenny sings like a pro" changes to "Kenny and his twin brother sing like pros." Notice the difference in the subjects and the corresponding changes in the verbs.

Rule 3

Indefinite pronouns attract singular verbs.

Indefinite pronouns are words such as *nobody*, *no one*, *anything*, *something*, *everywhere*, *nowhere*, *somebody*, *somewhere*, and other related words. These words do not refer to a specific person or object. Hence, they attract singular verbs. Consider some examples.

"No one knows tomorrow." Here, *no one* is the indefinite pronoun as the subject. According to the rule, it attracts *knows*, a singular verb. "Someone believes in you" and "Nowhere is safe" are two other examples of indefinite pronouns and singular verbs.

Rule 4

The principle of proximity

When you have more than one noun or pronoun as the subject, the principle of proximity will help you choose the most appropriate verb. The principle states that if you have more than one pronoun or noun as the subject, your choice of verb should be determined by the nearest pronoun or noun to the verb position. Consider a few examples.

"If he wins, his coach, his parents, or his friends deserve the applause." Here, there are three subjects: his coach, his parents, and his friends. The noun closest to the verb is *his friends*. Since this refers to more than one person, it attracts a plural verb. Remember, such verbs do not have an *s*. Therefore, the appropriate verb is *deserve*, not *deserves*. Let us change the order of arrangement of the subjects to see the impact on the verb.

"If he wins, his parents, his friends, or his coach deserves the applause." Did you notice any difference in the verb? The verb changed from *deserve* to *deserves*. Why? The closest subject to the verb is *his coach*. His coach is just one person, a singular subject. Hence, it attracts a singular verb as well.

Rule 5

A pair of attracts a singular verb.

When you come across *a pair of* in a sentence, the rule stipulates that the accompanying verb should be singular. Some examples are "A pair of scissors makes the work a lot easier." "A pair of trousers costs more than a pair of shirts." Notice that *a pair of* is accompanied by *makes* and *costs*, both singular verbs.

Rule 6

Mandative subjunctives attract plural verbs.

When words such as *wish, pray, recommend, suggest*, or *demand* are used in a sentence, usually when making a demand or suggestion, the accompanying verb must be plural, irrespective of whether the subject is plural or singular. Here are two examples:

"The board has recommended that the employee resign." The verb in this sentence is *resign*, a plural verb. The choice is made based on the word *recommended*.

"I suggest he take time off to recover." The same principle applies. *Suggest* influences the choice of verb, hence why *take* is the appropriate plural verb rather than *takes*, a singular verb.

Rule 7

Many a– attracts a singular verb and subject.

When *many a–* appears in a sentence, it should be followed by a singular verb and a singular subject.

"Many a boy loves football" and "Many a girl loves dancing" are two examples of how this rule can be applied in a sentence.

Rule 8

Collective noun concord

A collective noun is any type of single-word noun that is used to refer to a unit. Some examples of collective nouns are *audience, congregation, clergy, club*, and more. The rule stipulates that such nouns attract plural verbs.

"The congregation meet regularly" and "The football team have a good academy" are some examples of how this rule is applied. The former example can be broken down further into "The members of the congregation meet regularly."

Rule 9

Parenthetical statements

A parenthetical statement is a statement that appears in parentheses in a sentence. The parenthetical rule states that such a statement should be ignored when choosing a verb for the sentence. Sometimes, the parenthetical statement may be indicated with commas. The same rule applies.

"The manager, not the CEO, has the final say on the issue." Here, *not the CEO* is considered a parenthetical statement and thus has no impact on the choice of verb. "The teacher (not his students) understands the principle." Although *his students* is closer to the verb position than *the teacher*, it is not considered when choosing the verb form because it is in parentheses.

Rule 10

More than concord

This rule states that when *more than* appears in a sentence, the next number or word determines the verb. Consider these two examples:

"More than one boy is in the classroom." The number that follows *more than* is *one*. Being only one indicates that the accompanying verb should be singular. Therefore, the verb is the singular *is*.

"More than two boys are in the classroom." In this example, *two boys* is next to *more than*. This indicates that the verb should be plural. *Are* is used here, which is the plural of *to be*.

Rule 11

One of concord

The expression *one of* is always accompanied by singular verbs whenever it appears in a sentence. The expression *one of* can be translated as *one out of many*. The appropriate verb for *one* person or thing is a singular verb.

Consider this example: "One of the kittens loves custard and milk more than the others." The singular verb here is *loves*. In the next example, "One of the vehicles consumes more gas than the others," the singular verb is *consumes*. You should notice that *one of* is succeeded by a plural noun before the singular verb.

Rule 12

Pluralia tantum

Some nouns, known as *pluralia tantum*, are naturally plural with no singular form, even if they are a single object. Thus, most of these nouns have a final *s*, while some of them do not. Regardless of whether they end with an *s* or not, the next verb should be a plural verb.

Examples of such nouns include some school subjects such as physics, economics, and mathematics. Some games such as Chutes and Ladders, billiards, darts, and kittles are members of the group too.

Pluralia tantums also include *jeans, clothes, police, series, news, titles*, and some diseases such as *mumps, tuberculosis*, and *measles. Funds, wages, savings, fireworks, outskirts, thanks, arms*, and *earnings* are a few examples of nouns that naturally occur as plurals and go along with plural verbs.

Consider these two examples: "The series of accidents on the highway calls for concern." "Chutes and Ladders requires some degree of luck." Although *series* and *Chutes and Ladders* are seemingly plural, they are actually members of *pluralia tantums* and should be treated as singular.

Rule 13

Coordinate concord

The coordinate concord rule states that when *and* joins two words or phrases to form the subject, the sentence will attract a plural verb.

These are just two examples: "Boyo and Tricial attend the same school." "The mother and her daughter run the shopping mall." As you can see, the *and* indicates a plural subject. As earlier stated, such subjects attract plural verbs.

Rule 14

Mathematical facts

Mathematical facts, such as addition, subtraction, and multiplication, can be used with both singular and plural verbs. So, you can use either singular or plural verbs without breaking any rule.

Consider these examples: "One plus three is four." "One plus three are four." According to the rule, both expressions are correct. However, when writing, use either of the two alternatives and stick to it. That makes your writing consistent.

Rule 15

All concord

All concord is a bit technical because the choice of verb depends on the meaning of *all* in the sentence. *All* can mean either "all the people" or "everything." If it means "everything," the rule of indefinite pronouns applies. It attracts a singular verb. On the other hand, if it means "all the people," that is a plural subject and automatically requires a plural verb.

"All in attendance believe in the supernatural." Here, *all* means "all the people" and thus goes with a plural verb, *believe.*

"All goes wrong when those in charge give up their power." In this context, *all* means "everything." Hence, it goes with a singular verb, *goes.*

Rule 16

Either or neither

When two singular nouns are joined by *either* or *neither*, the verb must be singular. On the other hand, if *either* or *neither* joins one singular and one plural subject, the verb is determined by the subject closer to the verb. Here are two examples to clarify this.

"Either Dennis or Brian knows the place." The two singular nouns are *Dennis* and *Brian*, and these are joined with *either*. A singular verb is used.

"Neither Dennis nor Brian knows the place." The two singular nouns, *Dennis* and *Brian*, are joined with *neither*. So, the sentence has a singular verb.

"Either Dennis or his brothers know the place." Here, we have two subjects. *Dennis* is a singular subject, while *his brothers* is a plural subject. Joining the two subjects with *either* indicates the need for a plural verb.

"Neither Dennis nor his brothers know the place." Here, we have two subjects. *Dennis* is a singular subject while *his brothers* refers to a plural subject. Joining the two subjects with *neither* indicates the need for a plural verb.

Rule 17

Much or *most* accord

The choice of verb depends on which of the two is used. A singular or plural verb may accompany *most* in a sentence, depending on whether the sentence revolves around an uncountable or a countable noun. For countable nouns, the accompanying verb should be plural, whereas uncountable nouns take singular verbs. Consider the following examples:

"Most of the vehicles are in a bad condition." Here, *vehicles* refers to a countable noun. Hence, a plural verb is used. "Most of the time is spent on planning." In this sentence, *time* is an uncountable noun and thus attracts a singular verb.

On the other hand, *much* will go with a singular verb whenever it appears in a sentence. Consider this example: "Much of the time was wasted." The use of *much* in the sentence automatically calls for a singular verb.

Rule 18

Every + plural number

If *every* precedes a plural subject, the next verb should be plural. However, *every* without a plural number attracts a singular verb. Here are a few examples:

"Every five puppies need a comfortable home." The number *five* that comes after *every* indicates the need for a plural verb. Hence, the choice of *need* over *needs*.

"Every cat loves a caring owner." The *every* in this sentence is not succeeded by a number. Hence, the appropriate verb is singular: *loves*.

Rule 19

Plural number concord

When a sentence contains a unit or an amount, such as a percent or a specific number of hundreds, thousands, meters, etc. , the corresponding verb should be singular. Here are three examples:

"Three hundred dollars seems so small in comparison with three hundred thousand dollars." The verb in this sentence is *seems*. It is a singular verb.

"Five percent of his income goes into his retirement plans." Here, *goes* is the singular verb in the sentence. While *five percent* gives the impression of a big number, it is treated as singular and is thus accompanied by a singular verb.

"Twenty-five miles corresponds to 40 kilometers." In this sentence, *corresponds* is the appropriate singular verb in accordance with the rule.

Rule 20

Categorization concord

A collective name attracts a plural verb. Examples of such collective names are *the poor*, *the handicapped*, *the weak*, *the successful*, *the rich*, *the gifted*, and so on. Note that there is a distinction between a collective name and a collective noun.

"The rich leverage the power of networking."

"The poor believe in a change of fortune."

"The weak need every form of assistance they can get."

In each example, the collective name does not refer to a single person but an infinite number of people in a group. Hence, *the rich* refers to rich people generally, and *the poor* refers to all the poor people. Thus, the rich or the poor are treated as plural subjects and thus are accompanied by a plural verb.

Rule 21

Double title subject

The double title subject occurs when two subjects joined by *and* refer to the same thing or person. When this occurs, a singular verb should be used.

"Our principal and adviser supports my career choice." In this sentence, *our principal and adviser* refers not to two people but one. Hence, a singular verb is appropriate. Now, consider a switch.

"Our principal and the adviser support my career choice." Here, two people are referred to as indicated by the article *the* before *adviser*. In such a sentence, the subject is plural and should therefore attract a plural verb. Hence, the choice of *support* over *supports*.

Rule 22

Uncountable nouns concord

Uncountable nouns, as the name implies, are nouns that cannot be counted or quantified in numbers or units. Examples include *equipment*, *water*, and *information*.

The rule stipulates that uncountable nouns are always written as singular nouns, without an *s*. Hence, *informations*, *equipments*, *waters*, *evidences*, and the like are wrong. To pluralize such uncountable nouns, you can use *a piece of* or other words or expressions to pluralize them. Here are some examples:

"When I needed some information about America, I checked the web."

"Our company needs some pieces of equipment for the ongoing construction work."

"I need two glasses of water."

The above examples show how to pluralize uncountable nouns without adding an *s* to the nouns themselves.

This section is undoubtedly the broadest section in the test. Thus, since you have tons of topics to study and know before the test, start your preparation as soon as possible. Ensure that you cover all the topics in this section to equip yourself not only for the test, but for the possible responsibilities that await you on the police force.

The knowledge you gain from this section will also come in handy when you write reports. Without this knowledge, you may struggle to write clear reports or read reports, journals, or other sources of information that may help you have a successful career on the police force.

Chapter Four: Incident Report Writing

As a police officer, your job description may include incident report writing. Knowing how to write accurate reports is a sign of professionalism. With an accurate report, you can give a detailed account of an incident without omitting pieces of information that are crucial to the investigation.

The following are some requirements you must keep in mind when writing an incident report:

Chronological writing is recommended when writing narratives. Thus, you are expected to describe an incident in the order in which the events occurred. If you know the name of the suspect or victim of an incident, use it. Otherwise, refer to the suspect with a number (e.g., Suspect #4).

If you are reporting a property case, every affected item should be listed in the appropriate Property Section. Although similar items may be grouped together, report identifiable items separately to be as clear as possible. The report should also contain the estimated value of the entire property.

For reports involving properties, general terms are preferred. Thus, rather than report that an emerald necklace was stolen, your report should indicate that a piece of jewelry was stolen.

Sometimes, the subject of a reported case may be a transient or a tourist. You must obtain their personal information and local address, including their phone number, hotel name, room number, and other relevant pieces of information. The report should specify the specific time the subject will leave their local address as well as when they will arrive at their permanent address.

If there are eyewitnesses and victims who may relocate before the trial begins, their secondary telephone numbers and addresses should also be obtained and documented. Thus, the prosecutor can easily locate them through the provided information when they are needed.

For a report involving a juvenile, obtain the juvenile's parent/guardian information. If the juvenile is a student, obtain their school information as well. These pieces of information should be reported in the report's Subjects Section.

While these are basic requirements, specific cases have their own unique requirements you must include in your report. Some of these cases and their peculiar requirements will now be discussed.

Battery

This includes all forms of battery, such as ordinary or aggravated battery. When reporting battery, the incidents should be reported in chronological order. The testimony of the affected subjects should be included and well described.

The report should also include how the battery was perpetrated and the type of weapon that was used to commit the crime. The extent of the injuries sustained by the victim or victims should be described in detail. What is the condition of the victim(s)? What is the degree of their injuries? Do not omit the extent of the injuries. Also mention whether medical attention was administered to the victim or not. If it was, who administered it?

If your report includes a suspect, the relationship between the victim and the suspect should be established. Find out if the victim or any witness can identify the suspect, and include that piece of information in your report. If the suspect has a vehicle and their vehicle's license plate number is provided, report that as well.

Extortion

Extortion refers to the crime of threatening to injure someone, accuse them of a crime, or damage their reputation with the primary intent of gaining financially from such a threat. A threat may also be issued against someone to give up something against their will. Include the following pieces of information when writing an extortion report:

Describe the demands or threats made by the suspect. Were the threats or demands delivered to the victim? If yes, who delivered the threats or demands? What is the source of the information the suspect used to threaten the victim? Are the suspect's intentions known? If yes, include this in your report. If the suspect delivered the threat personally, did they come in a vehicle? If yes, what is the vehicle's license plate number? These pieces of information should all be covered in the report.

Homicide/Suicide

In this category are different types of unlawful killing. You must write a report about such a killing and include some valuable pieces of information in your writing.

Describe the crime's exact location. Include specific details of the house, car, street, or any other relevant information. What is the degree of injury sustained by the victim? Did the victim receive medical attention after they were found? If yes, who administered the medical assistance?

If it was a suicide case, how did you arrive at that conclusion? A detailed explanation will shed more light on the incident.

Abuse/Neglect

This section covers all types of abuse, ranging from child neglect and abuse to elderly neglect and abuse. The child abuse or neglect report covers incidents of neglect or abuse of individuals under the age of 18. The suspect is either a parent or their temporary or permanent guardian. On the other hand, the elderly neglect or abuse report covers incidents of neglect or abuse of individuals aged 60 years or older. The suspect could be a caregiver, relative, or another adult neighbor.

When reporting such an incident, include the specifics of the neglect or abuse. The report should also include how the crime was perpetrated, without excluding the details of the involvement of all suspects.

Did the victim sustain any form of injury during the abuse? If yes, describe the type and extent of the injuries. How was it inflicted? Has the victim received any medical attention? How long has the relationship existed between the suspect and the victim?

If you are listing the suspect, why do you consider the individual a suspect? Can witnesses or the victim identify the suspect? If the suspect has already been identified, what medium of identification was used? Was it through street ID or photo lineup? Who identified the suspect?

Arson/Attempted Arson

Arson is a crime that involves the willful destruction of a property by an explosive or fire. Arson may be committed on a private or public property for a wide range of reasons. When reporting arson, bear some important points in mind.

What type of structure was destroyed by the arson? Was the structure occupied at the time of the crime? Who are the residents, if any? If it is not a residential structure, find out if it is a business structure and determine if it was open at the time of the incident.

Try to identify the cause of the destruction, because it may be due to an explosion or fire not treated as arson. Your report should include the person who discovered the incident as well as the person who reported it.

What was the fire department's response to the incident? Record the unit name or number of the responding unit(s). If you want to list the suspect(s), establish the relationship between the suspect(s) and the victim. Your report must include why you consider an individual the suspect.

Report if the suspect has a vehicle or not. If the suspect does, describe the vehicle in full. If you have the license plate number, record this in your report. Also include the departments that were notified of the arson. This should include the fire department, the CID, and other relevant agencies.

Sexual Battery

This section covers how you should write incident reports on a wide range of sexual battery incidents. From sexual battery to attempted sexual battery, and armed sexual battery to attempted armed sexual battery, the following pieces of information should make it into your report.

How soon after the battery was the incident reported? If it was delayed, include the reason for the delay. The environmental condition should also be well described. This includes whether there was lighting in the environment where the crime was perpetrated or not. What about the victim's condition? Was the victim asleep or awake at the time of the incident? From which direction did the suspect approach the victim? Was there any discussion between the victim and the suspect before the attack?

If the suspect used force during the incident, describe the attack in your report. The description should cover whether physical violence was involved or not. Did the suspect use a weapon or threats? If the suspect used a weapon, describe the type of weapon and how the suspect used it.

The sex acts performed should be well described. If the victim sustained injuries during the attack, record the injuries and their extent. If the attack occurred in a vehicle or if a vehicle was involved, describe the interior of the vehicle, including any objects and other helpful details that may assist the police in identifying the suspect.

Aside from the sex acts and injuries, did the suspect take any items from the victim's home or the victim?

Kidnapping/Attempted Kidnapping

A kidnapping or attempted kidnapping case refers to secretly or forcibly taking someone against their will. The kidnapping may include threatening or imprisoning the victim with the primary intent of holding them for ransom or as a hostage.

Describe with as much detail as possible the condition of the environment where the kidnapping took place. Where was the victim last seen? Who saw the victim last and where? You should also report whether the suspect has contacted the authorities or the victim's family. If the victim's family has been contacted, what was the method of contact? Did the suspect make demands?

In the suspect's description, your report should provide detailed information on the relationship between the victim and suspect. How did you arrive at the suspect's identity? Was it through street ID or photo lineup? Or was the victim able to identify the suspect based on personal recognition? Describe the suspect's vehicle if applicable. The description should include the vehicle's registration information and other pieces of information that may be helpful in identifying the suspect.

Are there witnesses? Did you obtain statements from the victim and witnesses? If you did, include the statements in your report. Report all available pieces of evidence. How did K-9 respond to the crime notification? If the agency did, what is the name of the responding officer? What is the result of their response? All these pieces of information should be listed in your report.

Missing Persons

A clear case of missing persons should be reported. For a missing person report, it must first be established that it is not a case of kidnapping or abduction. Once that is confirmed, write a missing person incident report. The report should contain the following pieces of information:

Where was the missing person last seen? Who saw the missing person last? When the person was found, were they alone or with a companion? If the person was with a companion, who was the companion? You must also report what the mission person was doing when last seen.

If the missing person was in transit when last seen, where were they headed? Were there other people or vehicles in the vicinity? Do not forget to include this information in your report. A complete report should also include whether the victim or any witness can identify the suspect. Also, describe the suspect's vehicle, if any.

Report if there are witnesses or not. If there are, include the statements obtained from the witness and/or the victim in your report. You should also indicate whether K-9 responded. If it did, write down the name of the responding officer. What was the result of their response? And finally, if the missing person left a note, attach it to the report with a photo of the missing person obtained from their relatives or friends.

Recovered Stolen Vehicle

The documentation of recovered stolen vehicle is done with this report, especially, if the theft took place in another jurisdiction. Thus, while writing your report, include how the vehicle or license plate was located.

If a suspect is identified, what is the relationship between the victim and the suspect? You should also include evidence that incriminates the suspect. Then, how was the suspect identified? Who identified the suspect? Describe the suspect's vehicle if they have one.

Did the victim or an eyewitness give statements? Where was the vehicle stolen? Attach pictures of the stolen vehicle as well. If the recovered vehicle was damaged, describe the damage. Are there parts missing? Describe them in full too. Include any information about K-9's response and maintain a crime scene contamination list too.

Armed Robbery

The robbery covered in this section includes commercial robbery, home-invasion robbery, and car hijacking. This refers to any forceful taking of any property or money from another person through the use of violence, force, or assault. When reporting the commercial robbery of a business, both the business and the business owner should be listed as primary and secondary victims, respectively. Thus, the business is listed as Victim #1, and the business owner is listed as Victim #2.

Your detailed report should give comprehensive information about the incident. Describe the environment in detail. Also include any involvement of the subjects that make the principals list.

Did the suspect make any demands from the victim? If they did, take note of this using the suspect's exact quotes when threatening the victim. Describe the injuries sustained by the victims, including the extent of the injuries. Do not forget to describe the location of the robbery. A detailed description should include the street, room number, and any other relevant pieces of information about the robbery.

If the suspect used a weapon during the robbery, indicate this in your report. Mention the type of weapon used and the impact on the victim. If the victim was scared during the attack, how scared were they? Your report is incomplete without these little details.

Describe the suspect in detail too, starting from their relationship with the victim. Explain why the person is considered a suspect and if they can be identified by either the victim or any witness. The medium of identification should also be listed. Is it through photo lineup or any other means of identification? When describing the identification process, quote the statements made by either the witness or the victim.

Step-by-Step Guide on How to Write an Incident Report

The following step-by-step guide will help you write a detailed and accurate incident report.

The initial step is to get from the department the correct forms for the type of report you want to write. This is necessary because there are different protocols for different incidents and an appropriate report form for each type. To make a neat report, use word processing software such as Microsoft Word. Use a grammar and spelling checker such as Grammarly to refine your report and make it error-free.

Do not wait for days after the incident before you start writing the report. Do this as soon as possible after the incident. It is advisable that you write the report on the day of the incident. If, however, that is impossible, jot some important points down to form the basis for the report when you want to write it. This is to ensure that your report is as accurate as possible. Otherwise, you may forget some important points if you wait too long after the incident. The rule of thumb is that the report should be ready within 24 hours of the incident.

Include all the necessary facts. This should include the time of the incident as well as the location and date. When writing the location, be specific. Exact street address and other relevant information are very important and should be included. As the reporting officer, write your name and ID number in the report. If you worked alongside other officers, record their names too.

When writing your report, describe how you got to know about the incident. Did you get a call or stumble on the incident? If you were called, note when you received the call and describe it in detail.

When describing the incident, write the report in first person and from your own perspective. Include every important detail in the report, including quotes from the victims and witnesses. Describe your role as accurately as possible too. The description should include the strategy you used in handling the situation and whether you used any physical force.

Your report must be thorough and detailed. Detailed descriptions leave no room for misinterpretation by the public. Rather, it gives everyone a clear picture of an incident without making them read personal meanings into the report. For an accurate description, provide every piece of information you can about a suspect or victim, including their facial expressions, physical condition, and other features you might have noticed while investigating the incident. If there are rumors, do not report them as incidents you witnessed. Instead, report them as they are. It is pretty obvious that you cannot substantiate hearsay.

Using clear language is a must when writing a report. Do not hamper your reader with confusing language that hides the details rather than making them stand out. Legal and technical words should be limited, with a focus instead on using clear and concise expressions.

Do not submit your report without ensuring its accuracy first. Review the report and check for grammatical and spelling errors. If you find any, fix them before submission. Pay attention to the content too. Check that your report is as accurate as possible. If you unintentionally omitted some important points, edit the report to include them. You do not want to submit a badly worded or incomplete report.

Once you are done with the proofreading and editing, go ahead and submit the report to the appropriate department.

Although the different types of incident share some similarities in reporting, it is noteworthy that each type of incident has particular requirements. Thus, you can improve your overall knowledge of incident report writing by studying the requirements listed in this section and using them as a template when writing each report.

Test 1

Mathematics Test 1: Questions

(1)   The police department recovered $1,250 from Suspect A and $2,600 from Suspect B. How much did the department recover altogether?

(A) $3,950

(B) $3,750

(C) $4,000

(D) $3,850

(2)   When taking stock of his store after a burglary, Tony estimated $550 worth of items were missing. This was in addition to the $650 stolen from the cash register. How much did he lose to the burglary?

(A) $1,000

(B) $800

(C) $1,200

(D) $1,100

(3)   There are three prisons in a state. If the first prison has 349 prisoners, the second prison has 231 prisoners, and the third prison has 845 prisoners, how many prisoners are held in the state?

(A)   1,225 prisoners

(B)   1,250 prisoners

(C)   1,425 prisoners

(D)   1,450 prisoners

(4)   Between January and March 2019, 525 car thefts were reported across the country. What was the average number of car theft incidents per month in 2019?

(A)   155 cars

(B)   175 cars

(C)   150 cars

(D)   165 cars

(5)   Out of 1,245 convicted criminals in the state within the past one year, 347 of them have now been released. How many criminals are still behind bars?

(A)   678 criminals

(B)   587 criminals

(C)   898 criminals

(D)   788 criminals

(6)   About 10 minutes before his shift ends, a police officer receives an emergency call that takes him out of office for 42 minutes. How many minutes of overtime did he do?

(A)   24 minutes

(B)   23 minutes

(C)   42 minutes

(D)   32 minutes

(7)   If Officer Brian takes 4 weeks off work every year, how many weeks has he worked over the past five years?

(A)   240 weeks

(B)   220 weeks

(C)   260 weeks

(D)   280 weeks

(8)   Out of over 12,000 prison officers in the country, 1,250 serve in an administrative capacity only. How many officers work in other capacities?

(A)   10,700 officers

(B)   10,750 officers

(C)   11,000 officers

(D)   11,750 officers

(9)   Officer Jane's job requires her to drive 250 miles between Monday and Friday. What is the average number of miles she drives daily?

(A)   35 miles

(B)   45 miles

(C)   50 miles

(D)   65 miles

(10)   If Officer Jane in the question above maintains the regimen for a year and does not drive on weekends, how many miles would she have covered by the end of the year?

(A)   10,000 miles

(B)   11,000 miles

(C)   13,000 miles

(D)   15,000 miles

(11)   Some 1,200 road accidents were recorded across five highways in 2018. What was the average number of accidents per highway in 2018?

(A)   200 accidents

(B)   300 accidents

(C)   240 accidents

(D)   450 accidents

(12)   A police department has 100 officers. How many female officers are in the department if it has 63 male officers?

(A)   33 female officers

(B)   43 female officers

(C)   37 female officers

(D)   47 female officers

(13)   If each section of a police department has 10 officers, how many officers are there in 12 sections?

(A)   100 officers

(B)   60 officers

(C)   80 officers

(D)   120 officers

(14)   In an attempt to beef up the security of a crime-infested region, the police department decided to reinforce the department with 500 additional officers. If there are 20 police stations in the department, how many officers will be added to each station on average?

(A)   20 officers

(B)   25 officers

(C)   40 officers

(D)   35 officers

(15)   If 3 out of every 5 officers are promoted in a department with 15 officers, how many officers are promoted?

(A)   9 officers

(B)   6 officers

(C)   10 officers

(D)   12 officers

(16)   During a recent training exercise, two administrative officers and three other officers are selected from each of their respective sections. If there are three administrative sections and five other sections in the department, how many officers were selected for training?

(A)   20 officers

(B)   25 officers

(C)   21 officers

(D)   30 officers

(17)   If the average number of reported battery cases in a week is seven, how many battery cases will be reported in six months?

(A)   170 battery cases

(B)   175 battery cases

(C)   168 battery cases

(D)   180 battery cases

(18) If 2 out of every 50 women have suffered domestic abuse, how many cases of domestic abuse are likely to be reported out of 500 women?

(A)   50 cases

(B)   100 cases

(C)   20 cases

(D)   10 cases

(19) What is the average age of 10 suspects if their total age is 230 years?

(A)   25

(B)   22

(C)   23

(D)   30

(20) What is the average age of five prisoners if their combined age is 240 years?

(A)   45

(B)   50

(C)   48

(D)   52

Reading Test 1: Passages

This section tests your reading and comprehension skills. The following passages are designed to prepare you for the reading section of the Police Officer Selection Test.

Passage 1: How to Stem the Tide of Sexual Harassment in the Workplace

According to Health Careers, approximately 21% of Americans have at one time or another experienced sexual harassment at work. Four out of every five sexual harassment victims are women, the report claims. Sadly, 28% of victims of workplace sexual harassment do not report their experience out of the fear that they will not get the desired justice. How can this disturbing trend be controlled?

Here are some practical tips that can help potential sexual harassment victims and employers reduce the occurrence of this unfortunate experience in the workplace.

First, the perpetrator should be penalized: While addressing the issue of sexual harassment in the academic environment, the US National Institutes of Health recommended that once a case of sexual harassment is established, the perpetrator should be made to face the music. They should be fired and sued for their misdeed. To serve as a deterrent for others, they may also lose opportunities such as licenses, grants, and other industry benefits.

Employers should also put policies in place to address sexual harassment. Such policies should be designed to protect the interests and rights of sexual harassment victims. This smart move may succeed in reducing the cases of harassment from colleagues and bosses.

Employers should make an effort to educate employees on what constitutes sexual harassment. For instance, sexual harassment includes unwanted sexual gestures and jokes, making offensive remarks about someone's clothing, sending unsolicited nude images, or displaying other related pictures or sexually suggestive posters or objects. Once this is well defined, employees can guide their remarks and actions in order to comply with established rules and regulations.

Every organization must also establish harassment-reporting procedure that employees can use to report cases of harassment. This should include whistleblowing. This enables employees to report cases of sexual harassment they are personally aware of.

Employers should also conduct annual training for their employees. During the training, it must be emphasized that the organization has zero tolerance for sexual harassment. Remind them of existing policies that address this. The training should also explain what constitutes sexual harassment and how victims of such harassment can attain justice.

Employers should also review and update their complaint policy and procedure when necessary. They must be sure to encourage all to take advantage of the policy to rid the workplace of unscrupulous elements who want to take undue advantage of their colleagues at work.

Every employer has the responsibility of protecting their employees from sexual predators and abusers. Hence, employers should do everything within their capacity to protect employees from colleagues and superiors who may want to sexually assault them. That is an effective way to make employees safer at work so that they can concentrate on their jobs without being concerned about sexual harassment.

Passage 2: Why Is Juvenile Delinquency on the Increase?

Juvenile crime ranks among the biggest problems that the US government and US citizens have to contend with. According to the Office of Juvenile Justice and Delinquency Prevention, over 728,000 juveniles were arrested for various crimes, including rape, arson, murder, vandalism, larceny-theft, and aggravated assault, among other serious offences, in 2018 alone. This raises the question: "Why is juvenile delinquency on the increase in the United States?"

Researchers have attributed the following factors to the surge in juvenile delinquency across the country:

Drugs: There is a huge connection between drugs and crime. Most drug users and addicts are criminals. They fund their addiction to drugs with income from their criminal activities. Most take to crime if they cannot earn enough from their legal jobs to support such an expensive lifestyle. Thus, juveniles who take to drugs may also find themselves on the other side of the law in their attempt to earn enough money to sponsor their habit.

Poverty: Poverty is another important reason why many kids take to crime. They engage in theft and robbery to take care of their needs. As unemployment rates hit the roof and many parents lose their jobs, their children may be unable to contend with their new reality of scarcity. Hence, they do whatever it takes to meet their own needs, even if that involves taking to crime.

Media violence: The media's role in increasing the rates of juvenile crime in the United States cannot be overemphasized. It is estimated that an average child will be exposed to some 100,000 different violent acts and over 8,000 murders on television before they reach seventh grade. This massive exposure to crime at such a tender age will have a profound negative impact on the child.

Family life: Children who are raised in homes where crime is normalized will naturally have an affinity for crime. If either or both of the parents live on the proceeds of crime, their children will undoubtedly follow in their footsteps because they will not see anything wrong with the lifestyle they grew up in. This may massively contribute to the increasing number of juveniles who are criminally minded in the country.

Broken homes: Children who are raised in broken homes are also at risk of opting for a life of crime. Irrespective of whether the parents are separated or divorced or one of them has died, the absence of one of the parents may have a profound effect on the child. With only one parent working around the clock to pay the bills, a child may lack parental love, care, and guidance. This may prompt them to consider a life of crime, especially with seemingly loving gang members. As the gang members provide a substitute for family and make crime more attractive, the child may let down their guard and be lured into crime before they are aware of their decisions.

Reading Test 1: Questions

(1)   What fraction of Americans have experienced sexual harassment at one time or another?

(A)   1/2

(B)   1/3

(C)   1/5

(D)   2/7

(2)   Which of the following statements is true?

(A)   Approximately 3 out of 10 sexual harassment incidents in the workplace go unreported.

(B)   Approximately 5 out of 10 sexual harassment incidents in the workplace go unreported.

(C)   Approximately 9 out of 10 sexual harassment incidents in the workplace go unreported.

(D)   Approximately 2 out of 10 sexual harassment incidents in the workplace go unreported.

(3)   What does *face the music* mean as used in the passage?

(A)   To bear the consequences of their actions

(B)   To forgo some privileges

(C)   To see their dream come true

(D)   To be passionate about their intentions

(4)   What should be the primary objective of sexual harassment policies?

(A)   To attain justice for the perpetrator of sexual harassment

(B)   To attain justice for the victim of sexual harassment

(C)   To attain justice for the witnesses of sexual harassment

(D)   To attain justice for both real and imaginary sexual harassment

(5)   Which of the following pairs do not constitute sexual harassment?

(A)   Unwanted sexual gestures and jokes

(B)   Sending unsolicited nude images and jokes

(C)   Making sexual remarks about someone's clothing and touching them inappropriately

(D)   Sending lewd text messages and making dating proposals

(6)   What role does whistleblowing play in sexual harassment incidents?

(A)   It helps report cases of sexual harassment.

(B)   It helps punish perpetrators of sexual harassment.

(C)   It helps sanction individuals wearing provocative dresses.

(D)   It helps screen reports of sexual harassment in the workplace.

(7)   Why does each organization need to define what constitutes sexual harassment in their workplace?

(A)   It enables employees to have a clear idea of attitudes to avoid when dealing with the opposite gender.

(B)   It enables employees to have a clear idea of attitudes to avoid when dealing with their superiors.

(C)   It enables employees to have a clear idea of attitudes to avoid when reporting cases of sexual misconduct.

(D)   It enables employees to have a clear idea of attitudes to avoid when dating a colleague.

(8)   Stemming the tide of sexual harassment in the workplace is limited to putting an anti-sexual harassment policy in place. True or false?

(A)   True.

(B)   False.

(C)   It depends on the organization.

(D)   There are no specific rules on how to curb this menace in the workplace.

(9)   What is the significance of reviewing and updating a company's complaint policy?

(A)   It makes room for adapting the policy to the company's changing needs.

(B)   It ensures that the company hires professionals who can regulate interpersonal relationships in the workplace.

(C)   It enables the company to ensure regular reports of sexual harassment cases.

(D)   It helps everyone understand the company's dos and don'ts.

(10)   Keeping a workplace free of sexual predators and abusers is the exclusive responsibility of management. True or false?

(A)   True

(B)   False

(C)   Not in all cases

(D)   Sometimes

(11)   What does *zero tolerance for sexual harassment* mean as used in the passage?

(A)   The organization is nonchalant about sexual harassment.

(B)   The organization has passive interest in sexual harassment.

(C)   The organization leaves no room for sexual harassment.

(D)   The organization shows some level of tolerance for sexual harassment.

(12)   What awaits a sexual offender according to the U.S. National Institutes of Health?

(A)   The death sentence

(B)   Life imprisonment

(C)   The loss of their job and access to grants and licenses

(D)   None of the above

(13)   According to the passage, what does *unsolicited* mean?

(A)   Excessive

(B)   Suggestive

(C)   Unrequested

(D)   All of the above

(14)   According to the passage, define *juvenile*.

(A)   Relating to young people

(B)   Exclusively for older people

(C)   For teenagers only

(D)   None of the above

(15)   What indicates that juvenile delinquency is a serious issue in the United States?

(A)   The number of juveniles arrested for different crimes

(B)   The increasing number of road accidents caused by underage drivers

(C)   Child abuse stats across the country

(D)   The increasing number of children becoming teenagers

(16)   Why do most drug addicts take to crime?

(A)   Crime fuels their passion for addiction.

(B)   Crime funds their addiction to drugs.

(C)   Crime and drug abuse are rooted in poverty.

(D)   Drug abuse increases a criminal's efficiency.

(17)   What is the connection between poverty and juvenile crime?

(A)   Some young people who find it difficult to meet their financial needs see crime as the only way out.

(B)   All poor people are wired to take to crime.

(C)   Poverty is caused by crime.

(D)   There is no correlation between the two.

(18)   How much does media violence impact levels of juvenile delinquency?

(A)   It reduces juvenile delinquency.

(B)   It sensitizes people to the danger of juvenile delinquency.

(C)   It promotes juvenile delinquency.

(D)   None of the above.

(19)   Children of crime-inclined parents have the tendency to take to a life of crime. True or false?

(A)   False.

(B)   True.

(C)   It is a very complex situation.

(D)   It depends on the environment.

(20)   What impact can broken homes have on children?

(A)   Broken homes make it impossible for children to build their homes.

(B)   Children from broken homes may develop criminal tendencies.

(C)   Children from broken homes avoid crime at all costs.

(D)   Children from broken homes are always broke.

(21)   Which of these circumstances will likely result in children having criminal tendencies?

(A)   Coming from a broken home

(B)   Having criminal parents

(C)   Lacking parental care

(D)   All of the above

(22)   What attribute of criminal gangs make them appealing to potential members?

(A)   They are cruel.

(B)   They are wealthy and famous.

(C)   They are seemingly loving and generous.

(D)   They can defend themselves.

(23)   Which of the following can lead to a broken home?

(A)   The death of a spouse

(B)   Separation

(C)   Divorce

(D)   All of the above

(24)   How exposed to crime are kids below seventh grade?

(A)   They are slightly exposed.

(B)   They are barely exposed.

(C)   They are well exposed.

(D)   Their level of exposure cannot be determined.

(25)   What do you understand by *media violence*?

(A)   It is a type of violence propagated by the media.

(B)   It refers to making and advertising movies and similar mediums that promote violence.

(C)   It refers to anti-violence media campaigns.

(D)   None of the above.

Grammar Test 1: Questions

(1)   Which of the following sentences contains a misspelled word?

(A)   The little boy is happy.

(B)   The litle boy has a sense of humor.

(C)   She is a courteous girl.

(D)   Tony doesn't handle serious issues with levity.

(2)   Which of the sentences below contains incorrect punctuation?

(A)   The boys mother lives in the neighborhood.

(B)   There are two girls in the room: Tina and Debra.

(C)   What is going on here?

(D)   The examination is just around the corner.

(3)   Identify the odd one out from the list below.

(A)   The woman said: Where is the big dog?

(B)   The distinction between the two is crystal clear.

(C)   Is there any hope for the common man?

(D)   Punctuality is the soul of business.

(4)   Identify the correct option below. How many witnesses were at the scene of the accident?

(A)   There were five witnesses at the scene of the accident.

(B)   There were five witnesses at the scene of the acident.

(C)   There were three witneses at the scene of the accident.

(D)   There were four witness at the scene of the accident.

(5)   What is the victim's main attribute?

(A)   She is meticulous.

(B)   She is meticulus.

(C)   She is agile and weid.

(D)   She is atractive and has a good sense of humor.

(6)   Identify the misspelled word in the following sentence: *She is canterkerous and has a poor sense of humor.*

(A)   Canterkerous

(B)   Misspelled

(C)   Sense

(D)   Humor

(7) Which of the following words can replace the underlined phrase in the following sentence? *The convict is a dyed-in-the-wool criminal.*

(A) Experienced

(B) Hardened

(C) Belligerent

(D) Superfluous

(8) Which of the following is the opposite of the underlined word in the following sentence? *She is renowned for her industriousness.*

(A) Laziness

(B) Cuteness

(C) Superfluousness

(D) Indecency

(9) Select the most appropriate word to replace the underlined word in the following sentence. *The victim suffered a lacerated arm in the robbery.*

(A) Broken

(B) Cut

(C) Peeled

(D) Deformed

(10)   Rewrite the following sentence. *She said: The cute kittens are behind the door.*

(A)   She said: The cute kittens are beside the door.

(B)   She said: "The cute kittens are behind the door."

(C)   She said: "The cute kittens are beside the door".

(D)   She said; "The cute kittens are behind the door."

(11)   The sentences below have some misspelled words, except one. Identify the accurate sentence from the list.

(A)   She is highly inteligent and successful.

(B)   Nobody knos tomorrow.

(C)   Nobody knows tomorow.

(D)   None of the above.

(12)   What is wrong with the following sentence? *What a deserved victory.*

(A)   A missing apostrophe

(B)   A missing hyphen

(C)   A missing exclamation mark

(D)   A missing ellipsis

(13)   Correct the error in this sentence?

(A)   Replace the question mark with an apostrophe.

(B)   Change the spelling of *error*.

(C)   Replace the question mark with a period.

(D)   Leave the sentence as it is.

(14)   Rewrite the following sentence. *He counted, "one, two, three, four, five, six, seven, eight, nine, ten."*

(A)   He counted, "One, two, three, four, five, six; seven; eight, nine, ten."

(B)   He counted, "One, two … ten."

(C)   He counted from one two ten.

(D)   None of the above.

(15)   Which of the words below is a good replacement for the underlined word in the following sentence? *He is <u>belligerent</u>.*

(A)   Interesting

(B)   Attractive

(C)   Aggressive

(D)   Encouraging

(16)   Isolate the odd member of the list below.

(A)   Chris and Bella are a couple.

(B)   It was done intentionally.

(C)   It was an unexpected favor.

(D)   He couldn't acommodate them for too long.

(17)   What is the antonym of the underlined word in the following sentence?
His <u>altruism</u> is second to none.

(A)   Selflessness

(B)   Unselfishness

(C)   Selfishness

(D)   Generosity

(18)   Differentiate between *complement* and *compliment*.

(A)   *Complement* means "to complete something," while *compliment* means "to express appreciation for something."

(B)   *Compliment* means "to complete something," while *complement* means "to express appreciation for something."

(C)   *Complement* and *compliment* are synonyms.

(D)   *Complement* and *compliment* are antonyms.

(19)   What is wrong with *accomodation*?

(A)   It is missing a letter m.

(B)   It is missing a letter *o*.

(C)   It is missing a letter *d*.

(D)   It is error-free.

(20)   What is the difference between *favour* and *favor*?

(A)   *Favour* is the British spelling, whereas *favor* is the American spelling.

(B)   *Favor* is the British spelling, whereas *favour* is the American spelling.

(C)   *Favour* attracts singular verbs, whereas *favor* attracts plural verbs.

(D)   *Favor* attracts singular verbs, whereas *favour* attracts plural verbs.

Incident Report Writing Test 1

Report Sample 1

Case Number: AB07/04/21/3322

Incident: Vehicle Theft

Reporting Officer: Constable Henry Stone

Date of Report: September 12, 2020

Mrs. Rose Dandy approached me at about 1002 hours on September 12, 2020, to report her stolen vehicle. Mrs. Rose Dandy, who lives at 20 Highway Street, Illinois, said she drove to Highbrow Shopping Mall, some 10 miles away from her home, and parked her vehicle outside the mall at about 0925 hours. She reportedly couldn't find her vehicle when she left the mall at about 1000 hours. She then realized that her vehicle had been stolen within the short period of time she had spent inside the mall.

She described the vehicle as an ash-color 2015 Toyota Camry. It was registered in the U.S. with the registration number 7TRR412. The lost vehicle is estimated at $17,000. That is aside from some valuables she left in the vehicle, estimated at $1,000.

Mrs. Dandy claimed she didn't remember whether she locked the vehicle remotely or not. A survey of the crime scene showed no signs of forced entry, such as broken glass.

However, when I checked the CCTV installed in the parking lot, it captured a young man in his mid-20s with a hood covering his head, who walked toward the car, opened the car, and drove it away at about 0937 hours.

After obtaining a sworn statement from Mrs. Dandy, I entered her vehicle as a stolen vehicle into our database. I also entered the description of the young suspect into our database.

The suspect has a wide forehead, a pair of protruding ears, and a long and narrow nose. He is very bearded with a well-trimmed moustache over a medium-sized mouth with thin lips.

Incident Report Writing Test 1: Questions

(1)   How long did Mrs. Dandy spend inside the mall?

(A)   Mrs1 hour

(B)   30 minutes

(C)   15 minutes

(D)   35 minutes

(2)   What is the total loss recorded by Mrs. Dandy?

(A) $16,000

(B) $17,000

(C) $18,000

(D) $15,000

(3)   What is the time difference between when Mrs. Dandy realized the theft and when she reported the theft?

(A)   10 minutes

(B)   5 minutes

(C)   2 minutes

(D)   15 minutes

(4)   How far is the mall from Mrs. Dandy's house?

(A)   15 miles

(B)   12 miles

(C)   25 miles

(D)   10 miles

(5)   From the passage, what conclusion can you make?

(A)   Mrs. Dandy was careless with the vehicle.

(B)   Mrs. Dandy intentionally left the vehicle unlocked.

(C)   Mrs. Dandy was guilty of aiding and abetting.

(D)   Mrs. Dandy was at fault.

(6)   *Remotely* as used in the passage means what?

(A)   From a remote area

(B)   From a central location

(C)   With the vehicle's remote keyless system

(D)   All of the above

(7)   The vehicle was parked for how many minutes before it was stolen?

(A)   10 minutes

(B)   20 minutes

(C)   17 minutes

(D)   12 minutes

(8)   Guess the suspect's age.

(A)   Between 13 and 25 years old

(B)   Between 24 and 26 years old

(C)   Between 28 and 30 years old

(D)   Between 40 and 45 years old

(9)   Which of the following is not true about the suspect?

(A)   He has a wide forehead and wears a pair of glasses.

(B)   He has a long and narrow nose.

(C)   He is very bearded with a well-trimmed moustache.

(D)   He has a long nose and thin lips.

(10)   How will you describe Mrs. Dandy's response to the theft.

(A)   She acted promptly.

(B)   She made a slow response.

(C)   She was indifferent to the theft.

(D)   None of the above.

Mathematics Test 1: Answers & Explanations

(1)   (D) $3,850

The total sum of money recovered from the suspects is $3,850.

Money recovered from Suspect A: $1,250

Money recovered from Suspect B: $2,600

Total money recovered = money recovered from Suspect A + money recovered from Suspect B

= $1,250 + $2,600 = $3,850

Hence, the total sum recovered was $3,850.

(2)   (C) $1,200

Total cost of stolen items: $550

Amount of stolen cash: $650

Total amount lost to the burglary = total cost of stolen items + amount of stolen cash

= $550 + $650 = $1,200

Hence, Tony lost a total of $1,200 to the burglary.

(3)   (C) 1,425 prisoners

Number of prisoners in the first prison: 349

Number of prisoners in the second prison: 231

Number of prisoners in the third prison: 845

Total number of prisoners = number of prisoners in the first prison + number of prisoners in the second prison + number of prisoners in the third prison

= 349 prisoners + 231 prisoners + 845 prisoners = 1,425 prisoners

Thus, there are 1,425 prisoners in the state.

(4)   (B) 175 cars

Total number of stolen cars over three months from January to March: 525

Average number of stolen cars per month = total number of stolen cars over three months/3

= 525/3

= 175

Hence, an average of 175 cars were stolen per month within the given time frame.

(5)   (C) 898 criminals

Number of convicted criminals: 1,245

Number of released criminals: 347

Number of criminals still behind bars = number of convicted criminals – number of released criminals

= 1,245 – 347 = 898

Therefore, 898 criminals are still behind bars.

(6)   (D) 32 minutes

Time spent outside the office: 42 minutes

Time remaining before on his shift: 10 minutes

Overtime = time spent outside the office – time remaining on his shift

= 42 minutes – 10 minutes = 32 minutes

Hence, he did 32 minutes overtime.

(7)   (A) 240 weeks

Number of weeks in a year: 52

Number of weeks off in a year: 4

Number of working weeks in one year = number of weeks in a year – number of weeks off in a year

= 52 weeks – 4 weeks = 48 weeks

Number of working weeks in five years = number of working weeks in one year × 5

= 48 weeks × 5 = 240 weeks

Hence, he has worked for 240 weeks over the past five years.

(8)   (B) 10,750 officers

Number of prison officers in the country: 12,000

Number of administrative prison officers: 1,250

Number of officers working in other capacities = number of prison officers in the country – number of administrative prison officers

= 12,000 officers – 1,250 officers = 10, 750 officers

Therefore, 10,750 prison officers work in other capacities.

(9)   (C) 50 miles

Total number of miles driven between Monday and Friday: 250

Number of days between Monday and Friday: 5

Average daily distance covered = total number of miles driven between Monday and Friday/number of days between Monday and Friday

= 250 miles/5 days

= 50 miles/day

Hence, Officer Jane covers 50 miles daily.

(10)   (C) 13,000 miles

Total miles covered per week: 250

Number of weeks in a year: 52

Distance covered in a year = total distance covered per week × number of weeks in a year

= 250 miles × 52 = 1,300 miles

Officer Jane would have covered 13,000 miles in a year.

(11)   (C) 240 accidents

Total number of road accidents in 2018: 1,200

Number of highways sampled: 5

Average number of road accidents per highway = total number of road accidents in 2018/number of highways sampled

= 1,200/5 = 240

Hence, there was an average of 240 accidents per highway in 2018.

(12)   (C) 37 female officers

Number of officers: 100

Number of male officers: 63

Number of female officers = number of officers − number of male officers

= 100 officers − 63 officers = 37 officers

Thus, there are 37 female officers in the department.

(13)   (D) 120 officers

Number of officers per section: 10

Number of sections: 12

Total number of officers in the 12 sections = number of officers per section × number of sections

= 10 officers × 12 = 120 officers

Hence, the 12 sections have 120 officers.

(14)   (B) 25 officers

Number of reinforcements: 500

Number of police stations: 20

Average number of additional police officers in each station = number of reinforcements/number of police stations

= 500 officers/20 = 25 officers

Therefore, an average of 25 officers will be added to each station.

(15)   (A) 9 officers

Number of officers: 15

Number of groups: 15 officers/5 officers = 3 groups

Number of promoted officers in each group: 3

If there are 3 groups with 3 officers in each getting promoted, then:

Number of promoted officers in total = number of promoted officers in each group × number of groups

= 3 officers × 3 groups = 9 officers

Thus, 9 officers are promoted out of 15 officers.

(16)   (C) 21 officers

Number of administrative sections: 3

Number of selected officers per administrative section: 2

Number of administrative officers selected = number of administrative sections × number of selected officers per administrative section

= 3 sections × 2 officers = 6 officers

Number of officers selected from each other section: 3

Number of other sections: 5

Number of officers selected from other sections = number of officers selected from each other section × number of other sections

= 3 officers × 5 = 15 officers

Total number of selected officers = number of administrative officers selected + number of officers selected from other sections

= 6 officers + 15 officers = 21 officers

Thus, 21 officers are selected for the training altogether.

(17)   (C) 168 battery cases

Number of battery cases per week: 7

Number of weeks in a month = 4

Number of weeks in 6 months = number of weeks in a month × 6

= 4 weeks × 6

= 24 weeks

Number of battery cases in 6 months = number of weeks in 6 months × number of battery cases per week

= 24 weeks × 7 cases = 168 cases

Thus, 168 battery cases will be reported in 6 months.

(18)   (C) 20 cases

50 women = 2 abuse

500 women = x abuse

Cross multiply.

50x abuse = 2 × 500

Divide through by 50.

x abuse = 2 × 10 women

x abuse = 20 women

So, out of 500 women, 20 will report domestic abuse.

(19)   (C) 23

Combined age of suspects: 230

Number of suspects: 10

Average age per suspect = combined age of suspects/number of suspects

= 230 years/10 = 23 years

Hence, the average age of the 10 suspects is 23.

(20)   (C) 48

Combined age of prisoners: 240 years.

Number of prisoners: 5.

Average age of prisoners = combined age of prisoners / number of prisoners

= 240 years / 5 = 48 years.

The average age of the five prisoners is 48.

Reading Test 1: Answers & Explanations

(1)   (C) 1/5

According to Health Careers, approximately 21% of Americans have at one time or another experienced sexual harassment at work. That is approximately one out of every five Americans. Thus, 1/5 of Americans have experienced sexual harassment.

(2)   (A) Approximately 3 out of 10 sexual harassment incidents in the workplace go unreported.

Sadly, 28% of victims of workplace sexual harassment do not report their experience out of fear that they will not get the desired justice. This implies that approximately 3 out of every 10 sexual harassment incidents in the country go unreported.

(3)   (A) To bear the consequences of their actions

When someone is said to face the music, they are said to bear the consequences of their actions. In this case, it denotes a painful reward for a bad action. Thus, in the passage, sexual harassers should face sanctions for their sexual misconduct.

(4)   (B) To attain justice for the victim of sexual harassment

No matter the content of sexual harassment policies, their primary objective is to get justice for the victims of sexual harassment. Thus, such policies should reflect the desire to ensure that the violator does not go unpunished and justice is achieved for the victim.

(5)   (D) Sending lewd text messages and making dating proposals

Sexual harassment includes making unwanted sexual gestures or jokes. It also applies to sending unsolicited nude images and jokes, making sexual remarks about someone's clothing, or touching someone inappropriately. However, while it also involves sending lewd text messages, it does not include making dating proposals.

(6)   (A) It helps report cases of sexual harassment.

As pointed out earlier, about 3 out of every 10 acts of sexual harassment go unreported. This drastically reduces the number of sexual harassment victims who get the required justice. Through whistleblowing, more incidents of such harassment can be reported by a third party who witnesses the harassment firsthand.

(7)   (A) It enables employees to have a clear idea of attitudes to avoid when dealing with the opposite gender.

Many people are ignorant of what does and does not constitutes sexual harassment. However, if an organization spells out the behaviors and attitudes that are considered to be sexual harassment, employees will know which attitudes to avoid when dealing with their colleagues.

(8)   (B) False.

There is more to stemming the tide of sexual harassment in the workplace than just implementing an anti-sexual harassment policy. As pointed out earlier, employees need training to give them an idea of what constitutes sexual harassment. This is in addition to a whistleblowing procedure and regular policy reviews.

(9)   (A) It makes room for adapting the policy to the company's changing needs.

What constitutes sexual harassment may change from time to time. Rather than get stuck in an outdated policy that does not reflect the current trend, organizations do well to review their policies as and when necessary. This enables them to adapt such policies to current trends and their changing company needs in the area of sexual harassment.

(10)   (B) False

Keeping an organization or work environment free of sexual predators and abusers is not an exclusive responsibility of management. In actuality, it is a collective responsibility that should be shouldered by all. This will guarantee better results in combatting sexual harassment in the workplace.

(11)   (C) The organization leaves no room for sexual harassment.

The expression *zero tolerance to sexual harassment* means that the organization will not tolerate any form of sexual harassment from any member, irrespective of their status, age, or achievements. Nobody is exempt from the company's penalties for such behavior.

(12)   (C) The loss of their job and access to grants and licenses

The U.S. National Institutes of Health recommends that the perpetrator be fired and sued for their misdeed. To serve as a deterrent for others, they may also lose opportunities such as licenses, grants, and other industry benefits.

(13) (C) Unrequested

Unsolicited means "unrequested or given without permission." In the context used in the passage, it describes sending nude images to individuals who did not request them. This makes it a sexual harassment offence.

(14) (A) Relating to young people

Juvenile means "relating to young people." Thus, according to the passage, juvenile delinquency are bad habits and crimes committed by young people. The youth in this case includes teenagers and others who do not qualify as adults.

(15) (A) The number of juveniles arrested for different crimes

The number of juveniles arrested for different crimes indicates that juvenile delinquency is a serious issue in the United States. According to the Office of Juvenile Justice and Delinquency Prevention, over 728,000 juveniles were arrested for various crimes, including rape, arson, murder, vandalism, larceny-theft, and aggravated assault, in 2018 alone.

(16) (B) Crime funds their addiction to drugs.

Most drug users and addicts are criminals. They sponsor their addiction to drugs with income from their criminal activities. Most take to crime if they cannot earn enough from their legal jobs to support such an expensive lifestyle. Their criminal activities help them sustain their habit.

(17) (A) Some young people who find it difficult to meet their financial needs see crime as the only way out.

Poverty is another important reason why many kids take to crime. They engage in theft and robbery to take care of their needs. Children of parents who are struggling with poverty may do whatever it takes to meet their own needs, even if that involves taking to crime.

(18)   (C) It promotes juvenile delinquency.

It is estimated that an average child will be exposed to some 100,000 different violent acts and over 8,000 murders on television before they reach seventh grade. This massive exposure to crime at such a tender age will have a profound negative impact on the child.

(19)   (B) True.

Children who are raised in homes where crime is normalized will naturally have an affinity for crime. If either or both of the parents live on the proceeds of crime, their children will undoubtedly follow in their footsteps because they will not see anything wrong with the lifestyle they are accustomed to.

(20)   (B) Children from broken homes may develop criminal tendencies.

Children who are raised in broken homes are at risk of choosing a life of crime. Irrespective of whether the parents are separated or divorced or one of them has died, the absence of one of the parents may have a profound effect on the child.

(21)   (D) All of the above

Children from broken homes may develop criminal tendencies. The same can be said for children whose parents are criminals or cannot care for them. By seeking parental care from outside of their home or following in their parents' footsteps, such children may fall into a life of crime.

(22)　(C) They are seemingly loving and generous.

Criminal gangs are seemingly loving and generous. A child who craves these qualities may be attracted to criminals who seemingly display them. As the gang members provide a substitute for family and make crime more attractive, the child may let their guard down and be lured into crime before they are aware of their decisions.

(23)　(D) All of the above

A broken home may result from the death of a spouse, separation, or divorce. Most broken homes are the products of at least one of these factors.

(24)　(C) They are well exposed.

It is estimated that an average child will be exposed to some 100,000 different violent acts and over 8,000 murders on television before they reach seventh grade. This massive exposure to crime at such a tender age will have a profound negative impact on the child.

(25)　(B) It refers to making and advertising movies and similar mediums that promote violence.

Media violence refers to all forms of violence promoted by the media. This includes promoting violence-filled movies and other entertainment that may normalize violence among consumers, especially juveniles.

Grammar Test 1: Answers & Explanations

(1)　(B) The litle boy has a sense of humor.

In this sentence, *litle* is spelled wrong. The correct spelling is *little*.

(2)　(A) The boys mother lives in the neighborhood.

The above sentence lacks a punctuation mark. The *boys* in the sentence denotes possession or ownership. Hence, an apostrophe is needed to convey the right meaning. Thus, the correct expression is "The boy's mother lives in the neighborhood."

(3)　(A) The woman said: Where is the big dog?

The sentence above is the odd one out. While other sentences have the appropriate punctuation marks, this sentence is missing a pair of quotation marks. Since the sentence makes a direct quote of someone's speech, the correct expression is this: The woman said: "Where is the big dog?"

(4)　(A) There were five witnesses at the scene of the accident.

This is a test of your spelling and grammar knowledge. In the second sentence, a c is missing in *accident*. In the third, *witneses* is incomplete, missing an s, while the last option contains a singular word, *witness*. This is incompatible with *four*, a word denoting plural.

(5)　(A) She is meticulous.

This is another spelling test. *Meticulous*, *weird*, and *attractive* are misspelled in the other options. Only the first option contains the correct spelling of *meticulous*.

(6)　　(A) Canterkerous

The misspelled word in the sentence is *canterkerous*. The correct spelling is *cantankerous*. The other words in the sentence are correctly spelled.

(7)　　(B) Hardened

Dyed in the wool is an expression that means "unchanging in an opinion or belief." Thus, is the best fit for this context.

(8)　　(A) Laziness

This is a synonym/antonym test. *Industriousness* means "hardworking." Naturally, the opposite of hardworking is laziness. Hence, *laziness* is the closest antonym for the word in the sentence.

(9)　　(B) Cut

A lacerated body is torn or cut deeply. Thus, *cut* is the most appropriate word to replace *lacerated* in the passage. They are synonyms.

(10)　　(B) She said: "The cute kittens are behind the door."

The sentence is incorrectly punctuated. Option B shows the correct punctuation. Notice the use of quotation marks to quote the direct speech made by the subject of the sentence.

(11)　　(D) None of the above.

None of the sentences is correct. *Inteligent* is missing an *l*, while *knos* should be spelled *knows*. Also, *tomorow* is missing an *r*. Thus, all the sentences are incorrect.

(12)   (C) A missing exclamation mark

"What a deserved victory" is an exclamatory remark, evident from the *What a ...* at the start. Hence, it should have been written as "What a deserved victory!" The exclamation mark shows the feelings expressed in the sentence.

(13)   (C) Replace the question mark with a period.

The sentence is an imperative sentence giving a command, not an interrogative one. Hence, it must not end with a question mark, but rather a full stop or period.

(14)   (B) He counted, "One, two ... ten."

To avoid a lengthy sentence, an ellipsis comes in handy. Three periods (...) are commonly used to represent this punctuation mark. In printing or writing, an ellipsis is used to show the omission of words or letters.

(15)   (C) Aggressive

A belligerent person is someone who is aggressive and hostile. Thus, *aggressive* can replace the word in this sentence.

(16)   (D) He couldn't acommodate them for too long.

The above sentence is the odd member of the list. While the other sentences have no grammatical or spelling errors, *accommodate* is spelled wrong here as *acommodate*.

(17)   (C) Selfishness

Altruism means "selfless concern for others' well-being." Simply put, altruism is the same thing as selflessness. Thus, its antonym, or opposite, is *selfishness*.

(18)   (A) *Complement* means "to complete something," while *compliment* means "to express appreciation for something."

Complement and *compliment* are homophones. However, while *complement* means "to complete something," *compliment* means "to express appreciation for something."

(19)   (A) It is missing a letter *m*.

The correct spelling is *accommodation*. This has a double *m* and not a single *m* as written in the passage.

(20)   (A) *Favour* is the British spelling, whereas *favor* is the American spelling.

These are two different spellings of the same word. While the British prefer *favour*, their American counterparts prefer *favor*.

Incident Report Writing 1: Answers & Explanations

(1)   (D) 35 minutes

She parked her vehicle outside the mall at about 0925 hours and came out at exactly 1000 hours. That is exactly 35 minutes after entering the mall.

(2)   (C) $18,000

Mrs. Dandy lost her car, which is valued at $17,000, to the theft. She also lost some valuables estimated at $1,000. Thus, she lost a total of $18,000 to the robbery.

(3)   (C) 2 minutes

She came out of the mall at exactly 1000 hours to discover her vehicle missing. She approached the officer at 1002 hours to report the theft. So, there was a mere two-minute interval between her discovery and the report.

(4)   (D) 10 miles

Mrs. Dandy lives some 10 miles away from Highbrow Shopping Mall.

(5)   (A) Mrs. Dandy was careless with the vehicle.

From the passage, it can be inferred that Mrs. Dandy was a bit careless with her vehicle. According to her, she was not sure whether she locked the vehicle remotely or not. That singular act made the vehicle vulnerable to theft. The thief was then able to access the vehicle easily.

(6)   (C) With the vehicle's remote keyless system

Most modern vehicles come with a remote control. If you do not lock your vehicle manually, you can do it via the remote control. It does not literally mean from a remote area, although you can use the remote from a certain distance.

(7)   (D) 12 minutes

She parked the car outside the mall at about 0925 hours. The CCTV footage then showed a young man approaching the car, opening it, and driving it away at about 0937 hours. That was just 12 minutes after she parked the vehicle.

(8)   (B) Between 24 and 26 years old

CCTV footage showed a young man in his mid-20s as the robber. People in their mid-20s are between 24 and 26 years old.

(9)   (A) He has a wide forehead and wears a pair of glasses.

Nothing from the description indicates that the robber wears a pair of glasses. According to the passage, the suspect has a wide forehead, a pair of protruding ears, and a long and narrow nose. He is very bearded with a well-trimmed moustache over a medium-sized mouth with thin lips.

(10)   (A) She acted promptly.

It can be implied that Mrs. Dandy acted promptly. From the discovery of the incident to making an official report, it took her only two minutes. That was swift.

Test 2
Mathematics Test 2: Questions

(1)   A team of five robbers shared a spoil of $12,500 equally among themselves. How much did two of them receive?

(A) $5,000

(B) $5,200

(C) $5,500

(D) $6,000

(2)   If the average value of items stolen from a store is $235.50, what is the total value of 15 items stolen from the store?

(A) $3,520.50

(B) $3,500.50

(C) $3,532.50

(D) $3,620.50

(3)   If $230.50, $500.50, and $500 are recovered from three suspects, what is the sum of money recovered from them?

(A) $1,200

(B) $1,250

(C) $1,231

(D) $1,230

(4)   If the distance between a crime scene and the police station is 25 miles, how long will it take the response squad to arrive at the scene if they drive at 100 miles per hour?

(A)   20minutes

(B)   15 minutes

(C)   12 minutes

(D)   25 minutes

(5)   If $12,000 was recovered from the $15,000 stolen by a team of robbers, what percentage of the money was recovered?

(A)   80%

(B)   75%

(C)   70%

(D)   85%

(6)   It was discovered that 2/3 of juvenile delinquency occurs in children between 15 and 17 years old. What percentage of juvenile delinquency is this age group responsible for? Round to the nearest percent.

(A)   75%

(B)   60%

(C)   80%

(D)   67%

(7)   What is the average speed of an officer who arrived at a crime scene 40 miles away in 30 minutes?

(A)   80 miles per hour

(B)   100 miles per hour

(C)   60 miles per hour

(D)   120 miles per hour

(8)   In response to an anonymous call for assistance, the response squad arrested six members of an eight-man robbery gang. What fraction of the gang escaped?

(A)   1/4

(B)   2/3

(C)   4/5

(D)   1/3

(9)   During a trial, four out of the six-member panel voted in favor of the suspect. Express the number of votes against the suspect as a fraction of the number of panel members.

(A)   1/2

(B)   1/3

(C)   2/3

(D)   4/5

(10)   The police department successfully cracked 1,250 out of 1,500 cases over three years. What is their success rate? Round to the nearest percent.

(A)   80%

(B)   85%

(C)   83%

(D)   90%

(11)   While investigating a crime report, the police department discovered a fraud of $15,000,000. If 10% of the money was recovered on the spot, how much was recovered?

(A) $1,000,000

(B) $1,200,000

(C) $1,500,000

(D) $2,000,000

(12)   Crime stats show that 4 out of every 10 crimes are committed by women. What percentage of crime is committed by men?

(A)   65%

(B)   50%

(C)   60%

(D)   80%

(13)   In her report, an officer listed these items as stolen: mobile phone ($550), five pairs of pants ($500), and two pairs of shoes ($400). What is the total cost of replacing the mobile phone and a pair of shoes?

(A) $700

(B) $750

(C) $950

(D) $1,000

(14)   Going by the information above, what is the total cost of replacing two pairs of shoes and a pair of pants?

(A) $400

(B) $500

(C) $550

(D) $650

(15)   A court judgment commanded a suspect to refund the sum of $1,000,000 over a period of a year. How much will the suspect refund in six months?

(A) $50,000

(B) $500,000

(C) $800,000

(D) $600,000

(16)   A suspect is required by the court to pay $5,000 interest on a sum of stolen money per month for 24 months. What is the total interest amount in 24 months?

(A) $60,000

(B) $2,400

(C) $120,000

(D) $80,000

(17)   What percentage of $5,000 is $200?

(A)   5%

(B)   4%

(C)   7%

(D)   10%

(18)   A man recovered $5,000 from $10,000 he was owed by a debtor. What fraction of the debt did he recover?

(A)   1/2

(B)   1/3

(C)   2/2

(D)   2/5

(19)   What is 10% of $500,000?

(A) $5,000

(B) $55,000

(C) $50,000

(D) $75,000

(20)   Crime rates in a city dropped from 10,000 cases per annum to 8,000 cases per annum. What was the percentage drop in crime rates in the city?

(A)   25%

(B)   55%

(C)   20%

(D)   35%

Reading Test 2: Passages

Passage 3: Why Do We Need Community Policing?

Otherwise known as community-oriented policing, community policing refers to a "philosophy of full service personalized policing, where the same officer patrols and works in the same area on a permanent basis, from a decentralized place, working in a proactive partnership with citizens to identify and solve problems," according to Bertus Ferreira in "The Use and Effectiveness of Community Policing in Democracy." Simply put, it refers to the collaboration between the police force and the local community with a view to identifying people with criminal tendencies in the neighborhood. Why is community policing a smart move by the police?

Here are some outstanding ways community policing benefits both the police and the collaborating community:

It makes policing easier. Through the combined efforts of the police and the local community, policing becomes a collective responsibility shouldered by all. Thus, the community can complement the police's effort and make policing a lot easier for the police force.

It helps establish a good relationship between the police force and the community. Through collaboration, the police and the community can work together to stem the tide of crime in the community. Over time, the community and the police force can establish and sustain a mutually beneficial working relationship that helps them easily identify the major causes of crime.

It helps combat terrorism. Terrorism is a menace that plagues the world. Through community policing, each community can identify people with terrorism leanings and work together with the police to nip their criminal tendencies in the bud. The same approach also helps prevent targeted violence and its consequences.

It offers more resources. When the community is involved in policing, citizens contribute their resources to complement the police's resources to combat crime within the neighborhood. This is a big plus for the police, as they are better equipped to discharge their responsibilities than they otherwise would be with their limited resources.

It reduces crime rates. Communities that ally with the police record reduced crime rates compared to other communities, thanks to the youth who may have otherwise engaged in crime now being involved in the community's security efforts. When a significant percentage of a community is involved in protecting the community, crime rates will go down significantly.

Community policing makes early criminal tendency identification possible. This stresses prevention and, when necessary, supports timely intervention before criminal plans are executed. This not only spares the community the stress and pain of dealing with the aftermath of crime but also helps boost the community's security.

Passage 4: War on Drugs: Is It a Worthy Battle?

For decades, the United States has been at the forefront of the war on drugs. Since President Richard Nixon declared war on drugs in 1971, reports have shown that the United States spends over a whopping $15 million annually on drug eradication initiatives. What has been the result? Is the war on drugs a worthy battle?

The war on drugs has split opinion among experts. One school of thought believes that the war has failed to achieve its objective and should be abolished. Leading the campaign against the war on drugs is the Global Commission on Drug Policy. This group, consisting of business leaders and politicians, is calling for the decriminalization of drugs and recommends turning attention to treatment as the only viable solution.

In a statement released in June 2011, the commission declared that the war has failed woefully and the global community is facing the devastating consequences of this failure. Some facts on drug addiction seem to support their assertion. Consider a couple of them:

Quoting the National Survey on Drug Use and Health, the American Addiction Centers reported in 2017 that almost 20 million Americans aged 12 and above had issues with a substance disorder. The figure included adults who suffered from illicit drug use and alcohol use disorders. The report and the increasing volume of drugs, such as cocaine and heroin, on the market support the idea that the government has lost its war against drug use across the country.

Supporting this conclusion is a report by Vox. According to this source, the US government has spent over $1 trillion over the past 40 years in its attempt to clamp down on drug use. However, this has not produced the desired result, as the government still considers drug use one of the most serious problems the country has to contend with. This is in addition to the skyrocketing rate of drug-related violence, not only in America, but around the world.

However, a second school of thought is of the opinion that the war on drugs has been pretty effective. Bill Bennett, nicknamed the drug czar by President Bush in 1989, asserted that without the war, the situation would have advanced from bad to worse. He believes that letting up the pressure will worsen the situation, whereas increasing the pressure on drug use yields a positive result, since users are always aware of the consequences of their actions. This explains why some drug users quit their passion for drugs out of the fear of serious penalties from the government.

Reading Test 2: Questions

(1)   What is the primary objective of community policing?

(A)   Improved community security

(B)   Easier problem identification in a community

(C)   Division of labor among police officers

(D)   The Recruiting locals into the police force

(2)   Define community policing.

(A)   The collaboration between the local community and the police force for effective policing

(B)   The collaboration between the local community and the police force to draft policing regulations for each community

(C)   The amalgamation of the local community and the police force for recruitment exercises

(D)   The soliciting of financial assistance from the local community to support the police force

(3)   How does community policing boost a community's security?

(A)   It makes a community's security a collective responsibility.

(B)   It makes a community's security an exclusive responsibility of the community.

(C)   It makes a community's security a lot cheaper.

(D)   It makes a community's security a part-time responsibility of the police force.

(4)   How is community policing mutually beneficial for the police force and the local community?

(A)   It reduces crime rates.

(B)   It is a novel idea.

(C)   It involves the community.

(D)   It is the preferred choice of most communities.

(5)   How does community policing help with combating terrorism?

(A)   It helps the police identify individuals with terrorism leanings.

(B)   It helps the police identify groups with terrorism leanings.

(C)   It helps the police identify individuals and groups with terrorism leanings.

(D)   It helps the police identify individuals with anti-terrorism leanings.

(6)   Community policing reduces the cost of policing. True or false?

(A)   True.

(B)   False.

(C)   Some factors determine the impact it has.

(D)   The community determines the cost of policing.

(7)   Why does community policing reduce the cost of policing?

(A)   Because there are fewer criminals to deal with.

(B)   Because the community supports the police force with its resources.

(C)   Because the police and the community learn how to manage the available limited resources.

(D)   None of the above.

(8)   It is believed that community policing makes early crime identification possible. How?

(A)   The police have a smaller area to cover.

(B)   The police can use intel from the locals to easily identify a criminal.

(C)   All of the above.

(D)   None of the above.

(9)   What is the impact of involving youth in a community in its policing?

(A)   They are involved in the community's security efforts and will not want to undermine their own efforts.

(B)   Their involvement means they are given a natural antidote to criminal tendencies.

(C)   They can hold key positions in the police force.

(D)   They make no contribution to the community's security.

(10)   What does *nip their criminal tendencies in the bud* mean?

(A)   To discourage them from their criminal tendencies

(B)   To encourage them to have criminal tendencies

(C)   To put a stop to their criminal tendencies before they execute their thoughts

(D)   Not to care about their criminal tendencies

(11)   What does *a significant percentage of a community* mean as used in the passage?

(A)   A small number of people

(B)   A huge number of people

(C)   Fewer than 500 people

(D)   Fewer than 1,000 people

(12)   What is the overall benefit of community policing to the community?

(A)   Reduced crime rates and no aftermath of crime to deal with

(B)   Reduced police officers and no aftermath of crime to deal with

(C)   Reduced crime rates and a serious aftermath of crime to deal with

(D)   Reduced crime rates and significant aftermath of crime to deal with

(13)   What does *a big plus* mean according to the passage?

(A)   Increased numbers of police officers

(B)   Increased numbers of locals supporting the police's security efforts

(C)   An added advantage

(D)   The police will have more criminal activities to deal with

(14)   Which of the following US presidents started the war on drugs?

(A)   Ronald Reagan

(B)   Abraham Lincoln

(C)   George Washington

(D)   Richard Nixon

(15)   Which of the following organizations is against the war on drugs?

(A)   The Global Commission on Drug Policy

(B)   The Global Commission on Drug Regulation

(C)   The Global Commission on Drug Use and Abuse

(D)   The Global Commission on Drug Addiction

(16) When did the commission declare its stance that the war against drugs had failed?

(A) July 2015

(B) July 2011

(C) June 2015

(D) June 2011

(17) How serious is the impact of substance disorders on US youth?

(A) Almost 20 million Americans aged 12 and above had issues with a substance disorder in 2017.

(B) Almost 20 million Americans aged 12 and under had issues with a substance disorder in 2017.

(C) Almost 20 million Americans aged 12 and above had issues with a substance disorder in 2018.

(D) Almost 40 million Americans aged 12 and above had issues with a substance disorder in 2017.

(18) What makes many people believe that the government has lost the war on drugs?

(A) The increasing number of drug users

(B) The availability of drugs such as heroin and cocaine on the market

(C) Both A and B

(D) None of the above

(19)   What has the war on drugs cost the US government over the past four decades?

(A)   Over $11 trillion

(B)   Over $10 trillion

(C)   Over $1 trillion

(D)   Over $0.9 trillion

(20)   Which of the following people believes that the government's war on drugs is yielding positive results?

(A)   Bill Gates

(B)   Bill Bennett

(C)   Alexander Crowe

(D)   Sylvester Origami

(21)   The Global Commission on Drug Policy is made up of which groups of people?

(A)   Health workers and former drug addicts

(B)   Politicians and business leaders

(C)   Health companies and Non-Governmental Organizations

(D)   Rehabilitated drug abusers and health workers

(22) The skyrocketing rate of drug-related violence in America is a pointer to what fact?

(A)   The drug trade is a lucrative business.

(B)   Drug users are wealthy people.

(C)   The government is losing the war on drugs.

(D)   Wealthy people will fight against the government's efforts to clamp down on drugs.

(23) What does *skyrocketing* mean?

(A)   Declining

(B)   Increasing

(C)   Having the desired result on users

(D)   Having no impact on users

(24) The term *substance disorder* as used in the passage includes what?

(A)   Drug and alcohol abuse

(B)   Drug abuse and hoarding

(C)   Drug abuse only

(D)   Addiction to cannabis only

(25)　From the passage, what indicates that the government's efforts against drug use are yielding a positive result?

(A)　The increasing number of drug users

(B)　The increasing number of drug users who quit their addiction out of fear of penalty from the government

(C)　The skyrocketing rate of drug-related violence

(D)　None of the above

Grammar Test 2: Questions

(1) An apostrophe is a punctuation mark used for what purpose?

(A) An apostrophe is used for showing possession.

(B) An apostrophe is used for show possession.

(C) An apostrophe is used for showing possesion.

(D) An apostrophe is used for showing posession.

(2) Complete this sentence: *Fola is a beautiful lady;*

(A) She is also brilliant.

(B) He is also brilliant.

(C) They are also brilliant.

(D) She is also briliant.

(3) Differentiate between *hurt* and *hut*.

(A) *Hurt* means "to harm," while *hut* means "a small shelter."

(B) *Hut* means "to harm," while *hurt* means "a small shelter."

(C) *Hurt* means "to murder," while *hut* means "a small shelter."

(D) *Hurt* means "to harm," while *hut* means "a small vehicle."

(4)   Which of the following is a correct question?

(A)   What is the average of 6 and 8.

(B)   Whot is the average of 6 and 8.

(C)   What is the average of 6 and 8?

(D)   Whot is the average of 6 and 8?

(5)   The examination is a test of his what?

(A)   It is a test of his inteligence.

(B)   It is a test of his intelligence.

(C)   Its a test of his intelligence.

(D)   Its a test of his inteligence.

(6)   Choose the antonym of the underlined word in the following sentence.
Kelly is a _benevolent_ lady.

(A)   Beneficiary

(B)   Malevolent

(C)   Wealthy

(D)   Well-educated

(7)   What word can replace the underlined word in the following sentence? *The CEO is frugal.*

(A)   Thrifty

(B)   Meticulous

(C)   Benevolent

(D)   Wealthy

(8)   Bolu is what type of player?

(A)   Bolu is an amater player.

(B)   Bolu is an amature player.

(C)   Bolu is an amatuer player.

(D)   Bolu is an amateur player.

(9)   Identify the misspelled word in the following sentence. *Doctor Hanry is a renowned athiest.*

(A)   Athiest

(B)   Renowned

(C)   Doctor

(D)   None of the above

(10)   Identify the misspelled word: *She was seen dancing with her coleague at the missionary house.*

(A)   Coleague

(B)   Dancing

(C)   Missionary

(D)   None of the above

(11)   Correct the error in the following sentence. *Kira told her friend: I am going.*

(A)   Kira told her friend; I am going.

(B)   Kira told her friend; "I am going."

(C)   Kira told her friend "I am going."

(D)   Kira told her friend: "I am going."

(12)   Rewrite the following sentence: *I love bread tea and butter.*

(A)   I love bread, tea and buter.

(B)   I love bread, tee and butter.

(C)   I love, bread, tea, and butter.

(D)   I love bread tea, and butter.

(13)   Choose the correct sentence from the list below.

(A)   It was a well planned meeting.

(B)   It was a well-planned meeting.

(C)   The suspect camoflaged as a passerby.

(D)   The cheif architect is missing.

(14)   Rewrite the following sentence. *I am passionate about three things, movies, music, and football.*

(A)   I am passionate about three things: movies, music, and football.

(B)   I am passionate about three things – movies,

(C)   I am passionate about three things. Movies, music, and football.

(D)   I am passionate about three things (movies, music, and football).

(15)   The young widow is in what condition?

(A)   She is in a dilema.

(B)   She is in a dailema.

(C)   She is in a dilemma.

(D)   She is in a dillema.

(16)   What is the error in the following sentence? *He has not acknowledged the receipt of the letter.*

(A)   Acknowledged.

(B)   Receipt.

(C)   Letter.

(D)   It is error-free.

(17)   What part of a vehicle reduces the vehicle's speed or brings it to a stop when applied?

(A)   The break

(B)   The brake

(C)   The breake

(D)   The braeke

(18)   It is not advisable to wear what type of shoe while pursuing a suspect?

(A)   High-heel shoes

(B)   High-eel shoes

(C)   High-hill shoos

(D)   High-hill shoes

(19)   As a man, you should learn how to do this.

(A)   Not a tie

(B)   Knot a tie

(C)   North a tye

(D)   Not a tye

(20)   What is the distinction between *your* and *you're*?

(A)   The former is a contraction of *you are*, while the latter is a possessive adjective.

(B)   The former is a possessive adjective, while the latter is a contraction of *you are*.

(C)   The former is a pronoun, while the latter is an adjective.

(D)   The former is an adjective, while the latter is a pronoun.

Incident Report Writing Test 2

Report Sample 2

Case Number: AB08/06/21/3328

Incident: Burglary

Reporting Officer: Constable Tricia Henry

Date of Report: July 12, 2018

On Thursday, July 12, 2018, Mr. Mark Morrison, the owner of the store Sports Equipment at 1234 Madison Avenue, Chicago, called the police headquarters at 0700 hours to report that his store was broken into between 2100 hours on Wednesday, July 11, 2018, when he left the store, and 0700 hours on Thursday, when he came back to open the store.

A team of three officers—Kelly, Robin, and Tony—was dispatched at 0705 hours to visit the store for investigation. They started the investigation at 0720 hours upon their arrival at the store.

Mr. Morrison reported that the thief or thieves went away with some 5 pairs of Adidas shoes at $250 per pair, 15 branded jerseys at $100 per jersey, and about 50 pairs of socks, valued at $500. He estimated the value of the stolen goods to be $3,250.

During investigation, the team discovered some broken glass behind the store where thief or thieves apparently gained entry after breaching its security. Apart from the stolen goods, it was also discovered that $2,000 was stolen from the cash register, bringing the total loss to $5,250.

The team took a couple of pictures of the area where the store's security was breached and their entrance. Pictures of some of the goods that were scattered during the theft were also taken.

The victim has been given a case number and his report has been registered for subsequent action by the Anti-Robbery Squad.

The victim is a 45-year-old American male living at 128 Ivy Lane, Los Angeles. No suspect has been identified as of the time of registering the robbery incident.

Incident Report Writing Test 2: Questions

(1)   Why did the store owner report the incident on July 11 and not July 12 when the incident occurred?

(A)   He was skeptical about the police's response.

(B)   He initially thought it was an illusion.

(C)   The burglary took place overnight.

(D)   He was so shocked that he couldn't reach out to the police immediately.

(2)   Within what period of time did the burglary take place?

(A)   Between midnight and 0500 hours on Thursday

(B)   Between 2100 hours on Wednesday and 0500 hours on Thursday

(C)   Between 2100 hours on Wednesday and 0700 hours on Thursday

(D)   Between midnight and 0700 hours on Thursday

(3)   How long did it take the dispatched police officers to reach the scene?

(A)   30 minutes

(B)   40 minutes

(C)   15 minutes

(D)   22 minutes

(4)   What is the total worth of the stolen pairs of Adidas shoes?

(A) $2,500

(B) $2,700

(C) $1,250

(D) $1,350

(5)   What is the total worth of the stolen goods, aside from the pairs of socks?

(A) $3,000

(B) $2,700

(C) $2,800

(D) $2,750

(6)   What from the passage indicates that the thief or thieves forcefully entered the store?

(A)   The presence of some broken glass behind the store

(B)   The presence of some work tools behind the store

(C)   The presence of some bunches of keys behind the store

(D)   The presence of some broken wood behind the store

(7)   *Breaching* as used in the passage means what?

(A)   To bypass the store's security

(B)   To support the store's security

(C)   To boost the store's security

(D)   To overwhelm the store's security

(8)   What is true about the victim?

(A)   He is careless.

(B)   He is meticulous.

(C)   He is senile.

(D)   He is too outspoken.

(9)   What is your personal assessment of the thief?

(A)   He is an amateur thief.

(B)   He is a professional thief.

(C)   He did a poor job.

(D)   None of the above.

(10)   Replace *apparently* as used in the passage with the right word.

(A)   Obviously

(B)   Ignorantly

(C)   Unpredictably

(D)   Quickly

Mathematics Test 2: Answers & Explanations

(1)　(A) $5,000

Sum of spoil: $12,500

Number of robbers: 5

Amount received by each robber = sum of spoil/number of robbers

= $12,500/5 = $2,500

Amount received by two robbers = amount received by each robber · 2

= $2,500 · 2 = $5,000

Thus, two robbers received $5,000.

(2)　(C) $3,532.50

Average value of stolen items: $235.50

Number of stolen items: 15

Total value of stolen items = average value of stolen items × number of stolen items

= $235.50 × 15 = $3,532.50

Hence, the total value of the items stolen from the store is $3,532.50.

(3)　(C) $1,231

Money recovered from Suspect 1: $230.50

Money recovered from Suspect 2: $500.50

Money recovered from Suspect 3: $500

Sum of money recovered = money recovered from Suspect 1 + money recovered from Suspect 2 + money recovered from Suspect 3

= $230.50 + $500.50 + $500 = $1,231

The sum of money recovered from the three suspects is $1,231.

(4)   (B) 15 minutes

Distance covered: 25 miles

Driving speed: 100 miles per hour

Time taken to cover the distance = distance covered/driving speed

= 25 miles/100 miles per hour

= ¼ hours

Note: 1 hour = 60 minutes

¼ hour = ¼ of 60 minutes = 15 minutes

It will take them 15 minutes to cover 25 miles.

(5)   (A) 80%

Amount of money stolen: $15,000

Amount of money recovered: $12,000

% of recovered loot = (amount of money recovered/amount of money stolen) × 100

= ($12,000/ $15,000) × 100

Divide through until the fraction is simplified.

= (12/15) × 100

= (4/5) × 100

= 0.8 × 100

= 80

Hence, 80% of the stolen money was recovered.

(6)   (D) 67%

Two-thirds of juvenile delinquency cases were caused by the age group.

Convert this fraction to decimal and multiply by 100 to get the percentage.

= (2/3) × 100 = 0.666666666 × 100

= 66.666666 or 66.7%

The age group is responsible for 67% of juvenile delinquency cases (rounded to the nearest percentage).

(7)   (A) 80 miles per hour

Distance covered: 40 miles

Time spent: 30 minutes or 0.5 hours

Driving speed = distance covered/time spent

= 40 miles/ 0.5 hours = 80 miles per hour

Hence, his average speed is 80 miles per hour.

(8)   (A) 1/4

Number of gang members: 8

Number of gang members arrested: 6

Number of escaped gang members = number of gang members – number of gang members arrested

= 8 members – 6 members = 2 members

Fraction of escaped gang members = number of escaped gang members/number of gang members

= 2 members/8 members

= 1/4

Hence, 1/4 of the gang members escaped.

(9)   (B) 1/3

Number of panel members: 6

Number of members who voted in favor: 4

Number of members who voted against = number of panel members – number of members who voted in favor

= 6 members – 4 members = 2 members

To express this as a fraction: number of members who voted against the suspect/total number of panel members

= 2 members/6 members = 1/3

Hence, 1/3 of the panel voted against the suspect.

(10)   (C) 83%

Number of cases: 1,500

Number of successful cases: 1,250

Success rate = (number of successful cases/number of cases) × 100

= (1,250/1,500) × 100

Divide through to simplify the fraction.

= (125/150) × 100

= (25/30) × 100

= (5/6) × 100

= 0.83333 × 100 = 83.3

Thus, their success rate is 83% (to the nearest percentage).

(11)   (C) $1,500,000

Fraud amount: $15,000,000

Recovered percentage: 10%

Recovered amount = recovered percentage × fraud amount

Note that 10% is the same as 10/100.

Therefore, recovered amount = (10/100) × 15,000,000

= 0.1 × 15,000,000 = 1,500,000

Hence, $1,500,000 was recovered.

(12)   (C) 60%

Number of crimes: 10

Number of crimes committed by women: 4

Number of crimes committed by men = number of crimes − number of crimes committed by women

= 10 crimes − 4 crimes = 6 crimes

Percentage of crimes committed by men = (number of crimes committed by men/number of crimes) × 100

= (6/10) × 100

= 0.6 × 100

= 60

Therefore, 60% of crimes are committed by men.

(13)   (B) $750

Cost of stolen mobile phone: $550

Cost of stolen two pairs of shoes: $400

Cost of one pair of shoes = cost of stolen two pairs of shoes/2

= $400/2 = $200

Cost of replacing a mobile phone and a pair of shoes = $550 + $200 = $750

So, the total cost of replacing the two items is $750.

(14)   (B) $500

Cost of replacing two pairs of shoes: $400

Cost of replacing five pairs of pants: $500

Cost of replacing one pair of pants = cost of replacing five pairs of pants/5

= $500/5 = $100

Cost of replacing two pairs of shoes and one pair of pants = $400 + $100 = $500

So, the total cost of replacing those items is $500.

(15)   (B) $500,000

Amount of money to refund in a year: $1,000,000.

A year = 12 months.

6 months = *half* of a year

Thus, amount to refund in 6 months = $1,000,000/2 = $500,000

Hence, he will refund $500,000 in six months.

(16)   (C) $120,000

Interest amount per month: $5,000

Interest amount in 24 months = interest amount per month × 24

= $5,000 × 24 = $120,000

The suspect will pay a sum of $120,000 in interest over 24 months.

(17)   (B) 4%

Total amount: $5,000

Fractional amount: $200

Percentage of $200 out of $5,000 = (fractional amount/total amount) × 100

= (200/5,000) × 100

= (2/50) × 100

= 0.04 × 100

= 4

So, $200 is 4% of $5,000.

(18)   (A) 1/2

Debt sum: $10,000

Recovered amount: $5,000.

Recovered amount : debt sum = $5,000:$10,000

Divide through by $5,000.

= ($5,000/$5,000):($10,000/$5,000)

= 1:2

The man recovered just 1/2 of the debt.

(19)   (C) $50,000

Total amount: $500,000

To change 10% to a fraction, 10% is the same as 10/100.

10% of 500,000 = fraction × total amount

= (10/100) × $500,000

= (1/10) × $500,000

= 0.1 × $500,000

= $50,000

Thus, 10% of $500,000 is $50,000.

(20)   (C) 20%

Initial crime rates in the city: 10,000 cases.

Final crime rates in the city: 8,000 cases.

Decrease in crime rates in the city = initial crime rates in the city – final crime rates in the city

= 10,000 cases – 8,000 cases = 2,000 cases

Percentage drop in crime rates = (decrease in crime rates / initial crime rates in the city) · 100

= (2,000 cases/ 10,000 cases) · 100

= 0.2 · 100

= 20

Hence, crime rated dropped by 20% in the city.

Reading Test 2: Answers & Explanations

(1)   (A) Improved community security

The primary objective of community policing is to boost a community's security through the joint efforts of the police force and the local community.

(2)   (A) The collaboration between the local community and the police force for effective policing

Community policing, or community-oriented policing, simply refers to the collaboration between the police force and the local community with a view to identifying people with criminal tendencies in the neighborhood and nipping their nefarious activities in the bud.

(3)   (A) It makes a community's security a collective responsibility.

Through the joint efforts of the local community and the police, a community's security is not left to the police force only. Rather, it becomes a collective responsibility shouldered by the police force and the community.

(4)   (A) It reduces crime rates.

Community policing reduces crime rates. This is mutually beneficial for the local community and the police force because the community's security will receive a massive boost while the police force will have a reduced caseload to deal with. The police can thus use their resources for other important things.

(5)   (C) It helps the police identify individuals and groups with terrorism leanings.

Through community policing, each community can identify people with terrorism leanings and work with the police to nip their criminal tendencies in the bud. The same approach helps prevent targeted violence and its consequences.

(6)   (A) True.

When the community is involved in policing, it contributes its resources to complement the police's resources to combat crime within the neighborhood. This is a big plus for the police, as they are better equipped to discharge their responsibilities than they otherwise would be with their limited resources.

(7)   (B) Because the community supports the police force with its resources.

Policing cost is drastically reduced when the community provides the needed manpower and other resources the police force needs to be more efficient. This reduces the cost of acquiring such resources, making policing less expensive.

(8)   (B) The police can use intel from the locals to easily identify a criminal.

The locals understand their environment better than the police. They can also provide the police with credible pieces of information about people with criminal tendencies. Such information can assist the police in preempting a crime and taking the necessary action to prevent the crime from taking place.

(9)   (A) They are involved in the community's security efforts and will not want to undermine their own efforts.

When youth in a community are involved in the community's security, they are less inclined to work to undermine their personal efforts. The community will therefore have fewer cases of criminal activity to deal with. This in turn will boost the community's security.

(10)   (C) To put a stop to their criminal tendencies before they execute their thoughts

To nip something in the bud means to "halt something at an early age." Thus, to nip criminal tendencies in the bud means to take necessary actions to prevent people from carrying out their criminal plans.

(11)   (B) A huge number of people

Significant means "sufficiently great or noteworthy." Thus, a significant percentage is a huge number of something. In the context, it means a large number of locals in the community.

(12)   (A) Reduced crime rates and no aftermath of crime to deal with

Community policing will reduce crime rates in the community. The community is therefore spared the pain of dealing with the aftermath of a crime that results in loss of life or property. The community's security will improve drastically.

(13)   (C) An added advantage

In the context of the passage, *a big plus* means "an added advantage." The availability of more resources provided by the locals will boost the police force's manpower, helping them discharge their responsibilities with ease. This is an improvement from depending solely on their limited resources.

(14)   (D) Richard Nixon

President Richard Nixon started the US war against drugs in 1971. Since then, the country spends over a whopping $15 million annually on drug eradication initiatives as subsequent administrations build on the foundation laid by the 37th US president.

(15)   (A) The Global Commission on Drug Policy

A school of thought believes that the war has failed to achieve its objective and should be abolished. Leading the campaign against the war on drugs is the Global Commission on Drug Policy.

(16)   (D) June 2011

In a statement released in June 2011, the commission declared that the war has failed woefully and the global community is facing the devastating consequences of this failure. Since that public statement, the commission has spared no effort in ensuring that the country hears its loud voice condemning the clampdown on drug use.

(17)   (A) Almost 20 million Americans aged 12 and above had issues with a substance disorder in 2017.

Quoting the National Survey on Drug Use and Health, the American Addiction Centers reported in 2017 that almost 20 million Americans aged 12 and above had issues with a substance disorder.

(18)   (C) Both A and B

Many are of the opinion that the government is fighting a lost battle. Their assertion is based on the increasing number of drug users in the country and the availability of drugs such as heroin and cocaine in the market. Thus, people have easy access to hard drugs in spite of the campaign against their use.

(19)   (C) Over $1 trillion

A report by Vox indicates that the US government has spent some $1 trillion over the past 40 years on its fight against drug use in the country. However, this has not produced the desired result, as the government still considers drug use one of the most serious problems the country has to contend with.

(20)   (B) Bill Bennett

A second school of thought is of the opinion that the war on drugs has been pretty effective. Bill Bennett, nicknamed the drug czar by President Bush in 1989, asserted that without the war, the situation would have advanced from bad to worse.

(21)   (B) Politicians and business leaders

The Global Commission on Drug Policy consists of business leaders and politicians. The group is calling for the decriminalization of drugs and recommends turning attention to treatment as the only viable solution.

(22)   (C) The government is losing the war on drugs.

The skyrocketing rate of drug-related violence across the United States indicates that the government is losing the war against drugs. Supporting this conclusion is the availability of hard drugs to millions of users in the country.

(23)   (B) Increasing

Skyrocketing means "increasing, usually at a rapid rate." This is in reference to the increasing number of drug-related crimes committed by drug abusers across the United States and the rest of the world.

(24)   (A) Drug and alcohol abuse

The term *substance disorder* is a generic term that includes drug and alcohol abuse. It also includes the abuse or addiction to any other drug that may have a negative impact on the user.

(25)   (B) The increasing number of drug users who quit their addiction out of fear of penalty from the government

There is a belief expressed in the passage that increasing the pressure on drug use yields a positive result, since users are always aware of the consequences of their actions. This explains why some drug users quit their passion for drugs out of the fear of serious penalties from the government.

Grammar Test 2: Answers & Explanations

(1)   (A) An apostrophe is used for showing possession.

Option A is the only option in which *possession* is spelled correctly.

(2)   (A) She is also brilliant.

Since the subject is a female, this eliminates Option B. More so, the *is* verb shows a singular subject. This eliminates Option C. While Option D uses the appropriate pronoun and verb, *brilliant* is spelled as *briliant*. So, Option D is out of the equation.

(3)   (A) *Hurt* means "to harm," while *hut* means "a small shelter."

Hurt and *hut* sound similar. However, while the former means "to harm," the latter refers to a small shelter.

(4)   (C) What is the average of 6 and 8?

The correct answer is *What is the average of 6 and 8?* In Option A, the question mark is missing. Options B and D begin with *whot*, an incorrect spelling of *what*.

(5)   (B) It is a test of his intelligence.

Option B is the only correct sentence. In Option A, *intelligence* is missing an *l*. Options C and D begin with *Its*, a possessive adjective, rather than *It's*, a contracted form of *It is* or *It has*.

(6)   (B) Malevolent.

Benevolent means "good-natured or well meaning." Thus, its opposite is *malevolent*, meaning "spiteful or malicious."

(7)   (A) Thrifty

Frugal means "economical or sparing with regard to money." Hence, it is appropriate that it can be replaced with *thrifty*, a word that means "using resources or money carefully. Not wasteful."

(8)   (D) Bolu is an amateur player.

This is a test of your ability to spell *amateur* correctly. As you can see, the correct spelling is in Option D.

(9)   (A) Athiest

This is a spelling test. *Atheist* is misspelled as *athiest* in the sentence. All other words are spelled correctly.

(10)   (A) Coleague

This is another spelling test. *Coleague* is the misspelled word in the sentence. The correct spelling is *colleague*. Other words are spelled correctly.

(11)   (D) Kira told her friend: "I am going."

This is the only correct rewrite option. Options A and B use a semicolon instead of a colon to introduce the quote. Quotation marks are missing too in Option A. In Option C, the colon is missing.

(12)   (C) I love bread, tea, and butter.

Option C obeys every writing rule. The words are spelled correctly and appropriate punctuation marks are used. *Butter* is wrongly written with a single *t* in Option A. *Tea* is misspelled in Option B, while Option D misses a comma between *bread* and *tea*.

(13)   (B) It was a well-planned meeting.

This is a test of your knowledge of punctuation marks, specifically the hyphen. Option B uses a hyphen to create a compound adjective before the noun *meeting*. Without the hyphen, Option A is incorrect. *Camouflaged* and *chief* are misspelled in Options C and D, respectively.

(14)   (A) I am passionate about three things: movies, music, and football.

Here, your knowledge of punctuation is put to the test. If you can recollect, you introduce a list like this with a full colon. You can compare Option A with the other options to see the marked difference between them.

(15)   (C) She is in a dilemma.

Dilemma is misspelled in all the options except Option C. Notice that all the letters in the word are single except *m*. Option A uses a single *m*, Option B introduces an extra *a*, and Option D doubles the letter *l*.

(16)   (D) It is error-free.

This is an error-free sentence. All the words are correctly spelled, and the sentence is devoid of grammatical errors.

(17)   (B) The brake

The correct word is *brake*. While it is a homophone of *break*, the former is the part of a vehicle that reduces its speed or brings it to a halt when applied, while the latter means "to separate something into pieces through a strain or blow."

(18)   (A) High-heel shoes

This question tests your knowledge of homophones. While *heel*, *eel*, and *hill* are similar in sound, they obviously have different meanings. So, it is advisable to avoid wearing high-heel shoe while running. An *eel* is a type of fish while *hill* refers to a piece of land taller than everything around it.

(19)   (B) Knot a tie

Knowing the meanings and differences in *not*, *north*, and *knot* will come in handy here. While *knot* is a word meaning "to tie something," *not* is used to bring about negative meaning. *North* refers to one of the four cardinal points. Thus, you knot a tie.

(20)   (B) The former is a possessive adjective, while the latter is a contraction of *you are*.

While *your* and *you're* are often used interchangeably by some, they are actually different. The former is a possessive adjective used to refer to something belonging to someone you are directly addressing. The latter is a contraction of *you are*.

Incident Report Writing Test 2: Answers & Explanations

(1)   (C) The burglary took place overnight.

Although the burglary took place on the 11th, the store owner did not report it until the 12th because the burglary took place overnight. He was not at the store when it was robbed. Thus, he could not have made an on-the-spot report.

(2)   (C) Between 2100 hours on Wednesday and 0700 hours on Thursday

According to the incident report, the store owner closed for the day at 2100 hours on July 11 and discovered the burglary when he arrived for work at 0700 hours on July 12. The burglary took place during that period.

(3)   (C) 15 minutes

It took the dispatched police officers just 15 minutes to arrive at the scene. According to the report, the team was dispatched at 0705 hours to visit the store for investigation. They started the investigation at 0720 hours upon their arrival at the store.

(4)   (C) $1,250

Mr. Morrison reported that the thief or thieves went away with some 5 pairs of Adidas shoes at $250 per pair. Thus, the stolen pairs of Adidas shoes were worth $1,250 altogether.

(5)   (D) $2,750

The stolen items include 5 pairs of Adidas shoes at $250 per pair, 15 branded jerseys at $100 per jersey, and about 50 pairs of socks, valued at $500. Thus, aside from the pairs of socks, some $2,750 worth of items were stolen.

(6)   (A) The presence of some broken glass behind the store

During investigation, the team discovered some broken glasses behind the store where the burglar or burglars apparently gained entry to the store after breaching its security. Nothing else from the report suggests anything contrary to this.

(7)   (A) To bypass the store's security

Breaching as used in the passage means "to bypass the store's security." That was the only way the burglar or burglars could access the store unauthorized.

(8)   (B) He is meticulous.

A meticulous person pays attention to details. He was able to give a detailed account of the stolen goods and their worth. That requires some level of attention to detail without which such a report would not have been possible.

(9)   (B) He is a professional thief.

Only a professional thief could pull off such a theft with ease. He knew where to breach the store's security in advance and did a thorough job without leaving traces behind for the police.

(10)   (A) Obviously

Apparently as used in the passage denotes *obviously*. Without an alternative entry route, the area where the security was breached was the only place the thief or thieves could have gained access to the store. Thus, *obviously* can replace *apparently* as used in the passage.

Test 3

Mathematics Test 3: Questions

(1) If 30% of criminals are adults aged 50 and above, what is the ratio of younger criminals to the total number of criminals?

(A)   7:10

(B)   5:7

(C)   2:3

(D)   4:5

(2) During a robbery, a four-man robbery gang made away with $500,000. If they split the money equally, how much did each of the robbers make?

(A) $120,000

(B) $125,000

(C) $150,000

(D) $128,000

(3) During a failed robbery attempt, a team of robbers lost six out of their eight men. What percentage of the team was lost?

(A)   80%

(B)   70%

(C)   75%

(D)   60%

(4)   Some stats show that crime rates surge by 20% in the summer. If the average crime rate in winter is 5,000 crimes, what is the crime rate in the summer?

(A)   4,000

(B)   4,500

(C)   6,000

(D)   5,200

(5)   A big mall lost 70% of its cash to armed robbers. If the mall had $120,000 in cash, how much was lost to the robbery?

(A) $80,000

(B) $75,000

(C) $90,000

(D) $84,000

(6)   A gang of kidnappers demanded $1,000,000 ransom from their victim's family. The family succeeded in raising $750,000. What percentage of the ransom did they raise?

(A)   75%

(B)   70%

(C)   55%

(D)   80%

(7)　　Eight out of every 10 kidnapping cases within the past 10 years were solved. What percentage of the cases remain unsolved?

(A)　　80%

(B)　　85%

(C)　　70%

(D)　　20%

(8)　　Driving under the influence is responsible for 80% of auto accidents. If there were 5,000 cases of auto accidents within the past four years, how many of them were the result of driving under the influence?

(A)　　4,500

(B)　　4,200

(C)　　4,000

(D)　　4,800

(9)　　Kidnapping cases in 2018 were 20% higher than in 2017. If 2,000 kidnapping cases were reported in 2017, how many kidnapping cases were reported in 2018?

(A)　　2,800

(B)　　2,200

(C)　　2,400

(D)　　2,600

(10)   Stats show that 2 out of every 20 female robbery victims are sexually assaulted. If there were 500 female robbery victims within the last year, how many of them were sexually assaulted?

(A)   60

(B)   50

(C)   45

(D)   62

(11)   In 2019, there was a 20% drop in assault cases from the previous year. If 500 cases of assault were reported in 2019, how many assault cases were reported in 2018?

(A)   550

(B)   650

(C)   625

(D)   400

(12)   Three-fourths of robberies between 2015 and 2018 occurred in shopping malls. What percentage of robberies occurred in shopping malls within that period?

(A)   70%

(B)   60%

(C)   75%

(D)   80%

(13)   A suspect was ordered to repay a theft of $500,000. If 20% of the repayment should be made in bonds and the rest in cash, how much was paid in cash?

(A) $480,000

(B) $420,000

(C) $450,000

(D) $400,000

(14)   If an average of 5,000 vehicles are reported stolen annually, how many vehicles are reported stolen in five years?

(A)   20,000

(B)   2500

(C)   22,000

(D)   25,000

(15)   If the distance between County A and County B is 120 miles, how long will it take a response team to reach County B from County A if the team drives at 60 miles per hour?

(A)   3 hours

(B)   2 hours

(C)   1 hour

(D)   30 minutes

(16)   While in pursuit of a suspect, a response team covered 180 miles in three hours. What was the vehicle's average speed?

(A)   45 miles per hour

(B)   70 miles per hour

(C)   60 miles per hour

(D)   55 miles per hour

(17)   If 6 out of every 10 assaults are perpetrated by young men under 40 years old, what fraction of assaults are perpetrated by this age group?

(A)   3/5

(B)   4/5

(C)   2/3

(D)   2/5

(18)   The percentage increase in robbery and assault over the past five years is 25%. Express this figure as a fraction.

(A)   1/3

(B)   1/4

(C)   2/5

(D)   3/7

(19)   A robbery incident led to the loss of $2,000. What fraction of the $5,000 in the cash register was stolen?

(A)   3/5

(B)   2/5

(C)   5/7

(D)   1/2

(20)   To meet his bail, a man is expected to make a deposit of $15,000. If that is 1/3 of his bail, what is his bail amount?

(A) $50,000

(B) $45,000

(C) $30,000

(D) $5,000

Reading Test 3: Passages

Passage 5: How Credible Are Eyewitness Accounts?

Eyewitness testimony is one of the most important tools used by the justice system to discharge its duties without fear or favor. The system depends on eyewitness testimonies to gather the evidence it needs to ensure justice while handling cases. The evidence eyewitnesses provide can be used to identify suspected criminals, make charges, and eventually convict them.

However, over the years, some psychological scientists have challenged the accuracy of the testimonies provided by eyewitnesses. In recent years, too, the world has been shocked at the turn of events where people convicted of past crimes have been exonerated by developments in DNA evidence. This has put a question mark on the credibility of eyewitness testimony.

Eyewitness accounts are considered fallible because people are prone to making mistakes. Sometimes, an eyewitness's vulnerability to making mistakes may have a massive impact on their account. Regardless of an eyewitness's willingness to be unbiased and present their testimony as accurately as possible, they may forget seemingly insignificant details that can have a huge impact on the judgment. Sometimes, they may also misinterpret an event they witness and thus unwittingly provide a biased account that may also influence the judgment. Either way, their mistake may affect justice, either directly or indirectly.

In the past, incomplete or nonexistent forensic analysis contributed to a reliance on eyewitness accounts. In the pre-DNA era, many people were convicted of a crime based on eyewitness accounts. Recent reports show that over 350 people who were wrongly convicted have been exonerated by complete and more efficient DNA evidence, which is incompatible with the available pieces of evidence on which those people were falsely convicted. The reports show that about 245 of the convicted people were victims of misidentification, further confirming that eyewitness accounts are not absolutely credible.

The flawed eyewitness accounts have succeeded in penalizing innocent people while the actual perpetrators of the crimes walk free and may commit more crimes. Does this imply that eyewitness accounts are of no importance to the justice system? Far from it!

As previously mentioned, the justice system still depends on eyewitness accounts when making decisions. Such accounts have helped with the conviction of criminals across the globe. While the system may put some measures in place to check the credibility of information gathered from eyewitnesses, it is not going to fully jettison that source of information.

Passage 6: How to Prevent Substance Abuse

If you google "drug abuse," you will be overwhelmed with tons of negative information about addiction to drugs. In the United States, millions of people are hooked on one form of substance or another. Their existence is dependent on addiction to drugs, alcohol, or other substances in harmful amounts.

This problem is not limited to young people, as an increasing number of older people are experimenting with drugs. If that trend is not reversed, the number of adult substance abusers will increase in the near future. How can this problem be prevented?

Use prescription drugs moderately: Unlike harmful drugs, such as heroin and cocaine, prescription drugs or medications are beneficial if used moderately. As a user, ensure that you stick to your physician's prescription. If you use more than the recommended dosage, you may gradually become a substance addict, with the same potential side effects as someone addicted to hard drugs.

If you are a parent of children or adolescents, keep your prescription medication away from them. This is a practical preventive measure against the temptation to experiment with or abuse drugs. If your children have easy access to all your medications, they may unwittingly take to drugs.

Educate your kids: Some parents shy away from discussing sensitive issues, such as drugs, with their kids. Do not be that parent. Your efforts to prevent drug abuse at home should include organizing a comprehensive and informative training session for your children. Your discussion should center on what constitutes drug abuse and the potential impact of addiction on their physical and mental health.

As an adult, updating your knowledge about drug abuse will also enable you to resist the temptation to indulge in such a destructive act. As you share with your kids the information you learned from your research, you are equally reminding yourself of the need to keep off drugs.

Live a balanced life: Your lifestyle is another factor you should consider when trying to prevent substance abuse. It is not uncommon for some people to turn to drugs to deal with such problems as heartbreak, loss of unemployment, loss of a lover, and other problems. If you find yourself in such a situation, rather than consider drugs as the panacea to your problem, focus on the bigger picture that life offers you.

Seek assistance: Seek help from friends and relatives. And if necessary, consult an expert to assist you in overcoming whatever challenges you are facing. Their input and support will help you find a solution besides relying on substances.

You may seek professional assistance if you notice signs of mental illness that may trigger your reliance on a drug. This is necessary because drug abuse and mental illness are connected. Rather than trying to ease the pain with drugs, consider seeking professional support. It can offer you healthier, longer-term solutions that help you avoid substance abuse.

Reading Test 3: Questions

(1)   How important are eyewitness accounts to the justice system?

(A)   They provide the system with the evidence it needs to bring about justice.

(B)   The system relies solely on eyewitness accounts to make final decisions.

(C)   Their relevance is dependent on the jurisdiction and personalities involved.

(D)   They have an insignificant effect on the justice system.

(2)   According to some psychological scientists, are eyewitness accounts always credible?

(A)   Yes, they are always credible.

(B)   No, they are not always credible.

(C)   They are credible in some regions and not credible in others.

(D)   They are not credible enough to be significant.

(3)   What causes people to be skeptical about the credibility of eyewitness accounts?

(A)   The reversal of some previous judgments by more credible DNA test results

(B)   The increasing interest in science and technology

(C)   Freedom of expression

(D)   Hatred for the judicial system

(4)   How can a simple mistake affect the credibility of an eyewitness account?

(A)   It can have a huge positive impact on the account.

(B)   It can have a massive negative impact on the account.

(C)   It has zero impact on the account.

(D)   Its impact cannot be determined.

(5)   In the context of the passage, what does *unwittingly* mean?

(A)   Unintentionally

(B)   Intentionally

(C)   Insignificantly

(D)   Significantly

(6)   What does *prone to* mean, according to the passage?

(A)   Indifferent to

(B)   Affected by

(C)   Vulnerable to

(D)   Slightly under the influence of

(7)   How many ex-convicts have benefited from the more reliable DNA testing?

(A)   Over 400

(B)   Over 300

(C)   Over 350

(D)   Over 500

(8)   What percentage of the wrongly convicted people were victims of misidentification?

(A)   60%

(B)   50%

(C)   70%

(D)   55%

(9)   According to the passage, are eyewitness accounts totally unreliable?

(A)   Yes, they are totally unreliable.

(B)   No, they are not totally unreliable.

(C)   None of the above.

(D)   Both A and B.

(10)   What from the passage indicates that issues with eyewitness accounts are not absolutely the fault of the eyewitnesses?

(A)   Their willingness to be unbiased and present accurate testimonies.

(B)   The number of accurate convictions made based on eyewitness testimonies.

(C)   None of the above.

(D)   Both A and B.

(11)   According to the passage, how can the justice system get the best from eyewitness accounts?

(A)   By verifying eyewitness testimonies before making decisions based on them

(B)   By throwing eyewitness accounts into the trash bin without a second thought

(C)   By using eyewitness testimonies from older people only

(D)   By restricting acceptable eyewitness testimonies to those from eyewitnesses under the age of seventy

(12)   What is one of the dangers of flawed eyewitness accounts?

(A)   Criminals enjoy their freedom and may commit more crimes.

(B)   Criminals may be prosecuted later.

(C)   The criminal not convicted may suffer a troubled conscience.

(D)   All of the above.

(13)   What word can replace *biased* as used in the passage?

(A)   Prejudiced

(B)   Doctored

(C)   Perpetrated

(D)   None of the above

(14)   What does substance abuse involve?

(A)   Addiction to drugs, alcohol, and other substances in harmful amounts

(B)   Addiction to alcohol only

(C)   Addiction to drugs only

(D)   Addiction to some selected drugs

(15)   How prevalent is substance addiction in the United States?

(A)   Hundreds of thousands of people are addicted to substances in the United States.

(B)   Tens of thousands of people are addicted to substances in the United States.

(C)   Millions of people are addicted to substances in the United States.

(D)   Only a handful of people are addicted to substances in the United States.

(16)   Is substance addiction limited to young people?

(A)   No, it is not limited to young people only.

(B)   Yes, it is limited to young people only.

(C)   No, it is limited to older people only.

(D)   No one can determine its impact on young people.

(17)   Differentiate between cocaine and prescription drugs.

(A)   Cocaine is a harmless drug, while prescription drugs can be harmful.

(B)   Cocaine is less expensive than prescription drugs.

(C)   Prescription drugs are harmless if used moderately, while cocaine is harmful.

(D)   Prescription drugs are for general use, while cocaine is for people with special medical conditions.

(18)   When do prescription drugs become harmful?

(A)   When they are used by pregnant women

(B)   When they are used by people with heart problems

(C)   When they are abused

(D)   When they are used sporadically

(19)   How can parents protect their children from drug abuse?

(A)   By purchasing the right amount of cocaine for them

(B)   By indulging their cravings for any type of drugs

(C)   By keeping all medicines away from them

(D)   By teaching them the best sources of heroin and cocaine

(20)   Why do some people shy away from discussing drugs with their kids?

(A)   They believe their children cannot understand the topic.

(B)   They consider such topics to be very sensitive.

(C)   They wait until the children become adults before discussing drugs with them.

(D)   They consider it inappropriate to discuss drugs with anyone.

(21)   What should be included in your drug discussion with your children?

(A)   The dangers of drug abuse only

(B)   What constitutes drug abuse and the impact of addiction to such drugs

(C)   How to handle the effects of harmful drugs

(D)   The most effective antidote to drug addiction

(22)   Why do some people turn to drugs?

(A)   To beat boredom

(B)   To deal with a serious physical or mental problem

(C)   To showcase their strength

(D)   To show they are adults

(23)   *Panacea* as used in the passage means what?

(A)   A permanent solution to a problem

(B)   A temporary solution to a problem

(C)   Something of great significance

(D)   Something of small significance

(24)   To beat addiction to drugs, which of the following set of people can be of help?

(A)   Your family members

(B)   Your friends and colleagues

(C)   Medical experts

(D)   All of the above

(25) From the passage, what can you conclude about attempting to solve a problem through drug use?

(A) Drugs are effective for solving personal problems.

(B) Drugs are ineffective for solving personal problems.

(C) Addiction to drugs has little or no impact on the addict.

(D) All of the above.

Grammar Test 3: Questions

(1) *The police officer arrived at the accident seen as soon as he received a distress call.* Identify the error in the previous sentence.

(A) Accident

(B) Distress

(C) Seen

(D) Received

(2) One of the sentences below is incorrect. Which one?

(A) The pear of scissors lies on the floor.

(B) She is an incorrigible liar.

(C) The examination takes place tomorrow.

(D) The entertainer held everyone spellbound.

(3) What did you put in the fridge?

(A) I put a bottle of whine in the fridge.

(B) I put a bottle of wine in the fridge.

(C) None the above.

(D) Both A and B.

(4)   Identify the misspelled word in the next sentence. *He bought the time from the local store.*

(A)   Time

(B)   Local

(C)   Store

(D)   Bought

(5)   *Ken is a hary and tall man.* Identify the misspelled word in the previous sentence.

(A)   Ken

(B)   Hary

(C)   Tall

(D)   None of the above

(6)   Which of the following is the opposite of *hostile?*

(A)   Accommodating

(B)   Intelligent

(C)   Diligent

(D)   Insolent

(7)   Before a person who commits a crime is considered guilty under the law, such a person is treated as what?

(A)   A suspet

(B)   A suspect

(C)   A susspect

(D)   A suspekt

(8)   Differentiate between *mussel* and *muscle*.

(A)   The former is a human body tissue, while the latter is a mollusk with a shell.

(B)   The former is a mollusk with a shell, while the latter is a human body tissue.

(C)   The former is a human body tissue, while the latter is a mollusk without a shell.

(D)   The former is a mollusk without a shell, while the latter is a human body tissue.

(9)   What is the difference between *leek* and *leak*?

(A)   The former is a vegetable, while the latter is a hole where water can escape accidentally.

(B)   The former is a hole where water can escape accidentally, while the latter is a vegetable.

(C)   The former is a noun, while the latter is an adjective.

(D)   The former is an adjective, while the latter is a noun.

(10)   What does the man want to purchase for his computer?

(A)   Accessaries

(B)   Accesaries

(C)   Accessories

(D)   Acessories

(11)   *On September 13, 2018, the company's secretery was fired for his involvement in a multimillion-dollar fraud.* Identify the misspelled word in the previous sentence.

(A)   Fraud

(B)   Multimillion

(C)   Secretery

(D)   Company

(12)   *The ocean is losing a wide variety of species of wail.* Which of the words in the previous sentence is misspelled?

(A)   Wail

(B)   Variety

(C)   Ocean

(D)   All of the above

(13)   Rewrite the following sentence. *What a miss?*

(A)   What a miss.

(B)   What a miss...

(C)   What a miss!

(D)   "What a miss."

(14)   Rewrite the following sentence. *There are five boy's in the classroom.*

(A)   There are five boys' in the classroom.

(B)   There are five boys in the classroom.

(C)   There are five boys' in the classrooms.

(D)   There are five boy's in the classroom.

(15)   Rewrite the following sentence. *I love three things ... movies, books, and music.*

(A)   I love three things: "movies, books, and music."

(B)   I love three things: movies, books, and music.

(C)   I love three things. Movies, books, and music.

(D)   I love three things, movies, books, and music.

(16)   What is the distinction between *bite* and *byte*?

(A)   *Bite* means "to tear something apart with a cutting tool," while *byte* is a measurement unit of digital information.

(B)   *Byte* means "to tear something apart with a cutting tool," while *bite* is a measurement unit of digital information.

(C)   *Bite* means "to use teeth to tear something apart," while *byte* is a measurement unit of digital information.

(D)   *Byte* means "to crush something with a mechanical machine," while *bite* is a measurement unit of digital information.

(17)   Pick the odd one out of the sentences below.

(A)   The cat ate the sauce.

(B)   The cat ate the source.

(C)   It was a delicate issue that needed urgent attention.

(D)   The suspect was eventually convicted after a lengthy trial.

(18)   Spot the error in the following sentence. *The decision to vacate the premises was soulely hers.*

(A)   Vacate

(B)   Premises

(C)   Soulely

(D)   All of the above

(19)   What led to the victim's incapacitation?

(A)   She was injured from the waste down.

(B)   She was injured from the waist down.

(C)   She was injury from the waste down.

(D)   She was injury from the waist down.

(20)   What punctuation mark is missing from this sentence.

(A)   An apostrophe is missing from the sentence.

(B)   A colon is missing from the sentence.

(C)   An exclamation mark is missing from the sentence.

(D)   A question mark is missing from the sentence.

Incident Report Writing Test 3

Report Sample 3

Case Number: MO07/04/21/0022

Incident: Attempted Bank Robbery

Reporting Officer: Sergeant Billy Great

Date of Report: August 20, 2020

The police headquarters received a distress call from an anonymous caller at about 0800 hours on Friday, August 20, 2020. The caller claimed he was suspicious of an attempted robbery at the local bank.

In a swift response to the call, a five-man squad was dispatched to the bank. The team arrived at the scene at 0815 hours. Working in collaboration with the bank's security, the squad foiled the attempted robbery. During a face-off that lasted about 30 minutes, four of the robbers were arrested, while their leader managed to escape.

The suspect is a middle-aged man, about 6 feet tall. He is a muscular African American, approximately 240 lbs, with a scar running from his cheek to his chin.

He is a clean-shaven man with a full and well-trimmed beard, sprinkled with some grey hair. His bloodshot eyes are indicative of regular hard drugs or alcohol use. He has a wide nose and narrow nostrils that meet his full moustache over medium-size lips.

He has a large head with small ears, flat against the head. He wears earrings on both ears. Just below the left ear is a heart-shaped tattoo.

As of the time of his flight, he wore an expensive shirt over bright-colored slacks. He had a blue scarf tied round his neck, matching the color of his bracelets. He had three rings on each hand and a gold-colored wristwatch to match the color of the rings.

He walks with a distinct gait that can easily make him stand out from a crowd. He was last seen escaping the scene around 0845 hours in a black Ford truck.

Incident Report Writing Test 3: Questions

(1)   What does *an anonymous caller* mean?

(A)   A caller hiding behind social media to conceal their identity

(B)   An informer who refuses to reveal their identity

(C)   An informer with special privacy privilege

(D)   None of the above

(2)   How long did it take the police to arrive at the robbery scene?

(A)   25 minutes

(B)   20 minutes

(C)   35 minutes

(D)   15 minutes

(3)   How long did the face-off with the armed robbers last?

(A)   45 minutes

(B)   30 minutes

(C)   15 minutes

(D)   10 minutes

(4)   Which of the following is true about the escaped suspect?

(A)   He is tall and muscular.

(B)   He is slim and lanky.

(C)   He is stout and muscular.

(D)   He is of average size.

(5)   What is responsible for his bloodshot eyes?

(A)   A punch in the face

(B)   Long years of alcohol and drug use

(C)   Days of sleeplessness

(D)   All of the above

(6)   Describe the suspect in one word.

(A)   Self-important

(B)   Meticulous

(C)   Benevolent

(D)   Intricate

(7) Replace *distinct* with an appropriate word from the list below.

(A) Unmistakable

(B) Synonymous

(C) Special

(D) Cantankerous

(8) What from the passage indicates that the gang leader lives an opulent life?

(A) His expensive shirt and gold-colored wristwatch

(B) His mannerisms and physique

(C) His passion for robbery and distinct gait

(D) His slacks and heart-shaped tattoo

(9) What made it easier for the police to foil the robbery attempt?

(A) The robbers' willingness to surrender

(B) Their collaboration with eyewitnesses

(C) Their collaboration with the bank's security personnel

(D) Their willingness to give it their all

(10)   What is your assessment of the anonymous caller?

(A)   He made a significant contribution to the victory.

(B)   He was a lucky whistleblower.

(C)   None of the above.

(D)   Both A and B.

Mathematics Test 3: Answers & Explanations

(1)   (A) 7:10

Percentage of older criminals: 30%

Percentage of younger criminals = 100% − percentage of older criminals

= 100% − 30% = 70%

Ratio of younger criminals to total number of criminals = 70:100

Divide through by 10.

(70/10):(100/10)

= 7:10

Hence, the ratio of younger criminals to the total number of criminals is 7:10.

(2)   (B) $125,000

Total amount stolen: $500,000

Number of robbers: 4

Amount made by each robber = total amount stolen/number of robbers

= $500,000/4

= $125,000

Hence, each robber made $125,000.

(3)   (C) 75%

Total number of robbers: 8

Number of lost members: 6

Percentage of lost members = number of lost members/total number of robbers × 100

= (6/8) × 100

= (3/4) × 100

= 0.75 × 100

= 75

Hence, the robbery team lost 75% of its members.

(4)   (C) 6,000

Average crime rate in the winter: 5,000 crimes

The average crime rate in the summer = average crime rate in the winter + 20% of the average crime rate in the winter

20% of average crime rate in the winter = (20/100) × 5,000

= 0.2 × 5,000 = 1,000

Average crime rate in the summer = 5,000 crimes + 1,000 crimes = 6,000 crimes

Thus, the average crime rate in the summer is 6,000 crimes.

(5)   (D) $84,000

Amount in cash: $120,000

Amount lost to robbery: 70% of cash

Amount lost to robbery = (70/100) × amount in cash

= (70/100) × $120,000

= 0.7 × $120,000

= $84,000

The mall lost $84,000 to the robbery.

(6)   (A) 75%

Ransom demanded: $1,000,000

Ransom raised: $750,000

Percentage of ransom paid = (ransom raised/ransom demanded) × 100

= (750,000/1,000,000) × 100

Divide through to simplify the fraction.

= (75/100) × 100

= 0.75 × 100

= 75

Hence, the family raised 75% of the ransom demanded.

(7)   (D) 20%

Number of reported kidnapping cases: 10

Number of solved kidnapping cases: 8

Number of unsolved kidnapping cases = number of reported kidnapping cases − number of solved kidnapping cases

= 10 cases − 8 cases = 2 cases

So 2 in every 10 were left unsolved, which is 2/10 as a fraction.

Percentage of unsolved cases = fraction unsolved × 100

= (2/10) × 100

= 0.2 × 100

= 20

Hence, 20% of kidnapping cases remain unsolved.

(8)   (C) 4,000

Number of reported auto accidents: 5,000

Percentage caused by driving under the influence: 80%

Number of accidents caused by driving under the influence = (80/100) × 5,000

= 0.8 × 5,000 = 4,000

4,000 auto accidents were caused by driving under the influence.

(9)   (C) 2,400

Reported kidnapping cases in 2017: 2,000

Reported kidnapping cases in 2018 = reported kidnapping cases in 2017 + 20% of reported kidnapping cases in 2017

20% of reported kidnapping cases in 2017 = (20/100) × 2,000 = 400

Reported kidnapping cases in 2018 = reported kidnapping cases in 2017 + 400

= 2,000 cases + 400 cases = 2,400 cases

Therefore, 2,400 kidnapping cases were reported in 2018.

(10)   (B) 50

Number of reported robbery cases: 20

Number of sexual assaults: 2

Fraction of sexual assaults = number of sexual assaults/number of reported robbery cases

= 2/20

= 1/10 or 0.1

For 500 reported cases, the number of sexual assaults = 0.1 × 500 = 50

Thus, 50 out of 500 female robbery victims were sexually assaulted.

(11)   (C) 625

Number of reported assault cases in 2019: 500

20% of reported cases in 2019 = x

x = 500/0.8 − 500 = 625 − 500 = 125 cases

Number of reported cases in 2018 = 500 cases + 125 cases = 625 cases

Hence, 625 assault cases were reported in 2018.

(12)   (C) 75%

Fraction of robberies in shopping malls: ¾.

Percentage of robberies in shopping malls = fraction of robberies in shopping malls × 100

= 3/4 × 100

= 0.75 × 100

= 75

Hence, 75% of robbery incidents occurred in shopping malls within that period.

(13)   (D) $400,000

Repayment amount: $500,000

Repayment in bonds: 20% of repayment amount

Repayment in bonds = (20/100) × $500,000

= 0.2 × $500,000 = $100,000

Repayment in cash = repayment amount − repayment in bonds

= $500,000 − $100,000 = $400,000

Hence, $400,000 was paid in cash.

(14)   (D) 25,000

Number of vehicles reported stolen annually: 5,000

Number of vehicles that will be reported stolen in 5 years = number of vehicles reported stolen annually × 5

= 5,000 vehicles × 5 = 25,000 vehicles

Hence, 25,000 vehicles will be reported stolen in five years.

(15)   (B) 2 hours

Distance covered: 120 miles

Driving speed: 60 miles per hour

Time taken to cover the distance = total distance/driving speed

= 120 miles/60 miles per hour

= 2 hours

It will take them 2 hours to cover the distance.

(16)   (C) 60 miles per hour

Distance covered: 180 miles

Time taken: 3 hours

Average speed: distance covered/time taken

= 180 miles/3 hours = 60 miles per hour

The vehicle's average speed is 60 miles per hour.

(17)   (A) 3/5

Number of assaults: 10

Number of assaults perpetrated by the age group: 6

Fraction of assaults perpetrated by the age group = number of assaults perpetrated by the age group/number of assaults

= 6/10, or 3/5 in its lowest terms

Hence, the age group is responsible for 3/5 of all assaults.

(18)   (B) 1/4

25% = 25/100

Since they are both multiples of 5, divide the numerator and denominator by 5 repeatedly until it cannot be divided further.

Alternatively, might know that 25 is a factor of both, so you can divide by 25.

If you do, you will arrive at 1/4.

Hence, 25% is 1/4.

(19)   (B) 2/5

Amount of money in the register: $5,000

Amount of money stolen: $2,000

Fraction of money stolen = amount of money stolen/amount of money in the register

= $2,000/$5,000

Divide through by $1,000.

= 2/5

Hence, 2/5 of the money in the cash register was stolen.

(20)   (B) $45,000

Deposit amount: $15,000

Value of deposit amount: 1/3

Total bail amount = deposit amount × 3

= $15,000 × 3

= $45,000

Thus, the bail amount is $45,000.

Reading Test 3: Answers & Explanations

(1)   (A) They provide the system with the evidence it needs to bring about justice.

Eyewitness testimony is one of the most important tools used by the justice system to discharge its duties without fear or favor. The system depends on eyewitness testimonies to gather the evidence it needs to ensure justice while handling case.

(2)   (B) No, they are not always credible.

While eyewitness testimonies have proven to be invaluable to the justice system, some psychological scientists have reservations about using eyewitness accounts. The accuracy of the eyewitness testimonies provided over the years has been challenged with DNA evidence and sometimes found to be false.

(3)   (A) The reversal of some previous judgments by more credible DNA test results

In recent years, the world has been shocked at the turn of events where people convicted of past crimes have been exonerated by developments in DNA evidence. This has put a question mark on the credibility of eyewitness testimony.

(4)   (B) It can have a massive negative impact on the account.

Sometimes, eyewitnesses may misinterpret an event they witness and thus unwittingly provide a biased account that may influence the judgment. Furthermore, they may also forget seemingly insignificant details that can affect a judgment.

(5)   (A) Unintentionally

According to the passage, *unwittingly* means "unintentionally." It reflects the accidental misinterpretation of an event that unintentionally provides a biased account that may influence a judgment.

(6)   (C) Vulnerable to

Prone to is synonymous with "vulnerable to." The text highlights the important fact that people are imperfect and can make mistakes. Sometimes, though, such mistakes can be costly as they may sway judgment in the wrong direction.

(7)   (C) Over 350 ex

Recent reports show that over 350 people who were wrongly convicted have been exonerated by complete and more efficient DNA evidence, which is incompatible with the available pieces of evidence on which those people were falsely convicted.

(8)   (C) 70%

Reports show that about 245 of the convicted people were victims of misidentification, further confirming that eyewitness accounts are not absolutely credible. This represents some 70% of the 350 people exonerated by DNA test results.

(9)   (B) No, they are not totally unreliable.

The justice system still depends on eyewitness accounts when making decisions. Such accounts have helped with the conviction of criminals across the globe. Thus, in spite of its shortcomings, eyewitness testimony still remains crucial to the success of the justice system.

(10)　(A) Their willingness to be unbiased and present accurate testimonies.

Regardless of an eyewitness's willingness to be unbiased and present their testimony as accurately as possible, they may forget seemingly insignificant details that can have a huge impact on the judgment. Thus, they are not absolutely at fault.

(11)　(A) By verifying eyewitness testimonies before making decisions based on them

The system may put some measures in place to check the credibility of information gathered from eyewitnesses. It can do this by subjecting every eyewitness account to a verification process before it is accepted in court.

(12)　(A) Criminals enjoy their freedom and may commit more crimes.

Flawed eyewitness accounts have succeeded in penalizing innocent people while the actual perpetrators of the crimes walk free and may commit more crimes.

(13)　(A) Prejudiced

Biased is synonymous with *prejudiced*. When used in the passage, it conveys the idea that not all eyewitnesses who provide flawed accounts do so deliberately. Some are unbiased and are just victims of forgetfulness.

(14)　(A) Addiction to drugs, alcohol, and other substances in harmful amounts

Substance abuse encompasses addiction to any type of hard drugs. It also includes alcohol abuse or addiction to other drugs, such as heroin, cannabis, and a wide range of others.

(15)　(C) Millions of people are addicted to substances in the United States.

In the United States, millions of people are hooked on one form of substance or another. This makes it a very serious issue for the country.

(16)   (A) No, it is not limited to young people only.

Substance addiction is a general problem that is not limited to young people only. An increasing number of older people are experimenting with drugs too. So, substance addiction is not limited by age, gender, or status.

(17)   (C) Prescription drugs are harmless if used moderately, while cocaine is harmful.

Unlike harmful drugs, such as heroin and cocaine, prescription drugs or medications are beneficial if used moderately. After all, they are used to cure a wide range of medical problems.

(18)   (C) When they are abused

If prescription drugs are abused, they can have a damaging impact on the abuser, similar to hard drugs. No wonder doctors and prescription drug manufacturers advise patients to use prescription drugs strictly as recommended by the manufacturer or a physician.

(19)   (C) By keeping all medicines away from them

If you are a parent of children or adolescents, keep your prescription medication away from them. This is a practical preventive measure against drug abuse temptation. However, if your children have easy access to all your medications, they may unwittingly take to drugs.

(20)   (B) They consider such topics to be very sensitive.

Some parents shy away from discussing sensitive issues such as drugs with their kids. Do not be that parent. Your efforts to prevent drug abuse at home should include organizing a comprehensive and informative training session for your children.

(21)   (B) What constitutes drug abuse and the impact of addiction to such drugs

Rather than shy away from discussing drugs with your kids, you should center on what constitutes drug abuse and the potential impact that addiction has on their physical and mental health.

(22)   (B) To deal with a serious physical or mental problem

It is not uncommon for some people to turn to drugs to deal with such problems as heartbreak, loss of employment, loss of a lover, and other problems. The reality, though, is that drugs are not a cure for such problems.

(23)   (A) A permanent solution to a problem

When used in the passage, *panacea* means "a permanent solution to a problem." It is in reference to those who turn to alcohol or drugs as the solution to their problems when going through a difficult time.

(24)   (D) All of the above

Seek assistance from friends and relatives. And if necessary, consult an expert to assist you in overcoming whatever challenges you are facing. Their input and support will help you find a long-term solution other than relying on substances.

(25)   (B) Drugs are ineffective for solving personal problems.

Turning to drugs or alcohol is not the best way to handle personal problems. Rather than getting help solving such problems, you may gradually become overdependent on such substances. This is the perfect recipe for drug/alcohol abuse or addiction.

Grammar Test 3: Answers & Explanations

(1)   (C) Seen

The error in the sentence is *seen*. It is confused with the appropriate word, *scene*. All other words are correctly written.

(2)   (A) The pear of scissors lies on the floor.

The word *pear* is used incorrectly to replace *pair*, the appropriate word. Thus, you have *a pair of scissors* not *a pear of scissors*. A pear is a type of edible fruit.

(3)   (B) I put a bottle of wine in the fridge.

Compare Options A and B. The difference between the two is *whine* and *wine*. While the former is a long, complaining cry, the latter is an alcoholic drink.

(4)   (A) Time

The misspelled word in the sentence is *time*. Considering the context, he bought a seasoning from the local store. Obviously, he bought thyme, not time.

(5)   (B) Hary

The misspelled word is *hary*. The context indicates that the writer is describing Ken. Hence, the appropriate word is *hairy*, not *hary*. The former shows that Ken has hair all over his body, while the latter word does not exist.

(6)   (A) Accommodating

A hostile person has no room for others. They are aggressive and have zero tolerance for anyone. On the other hand, an accommodating person is the very opposite of a hostile person. Hence, *accommodating* is the opposite of *hostile*.

(7)   (B) A suspect

Option B is the correct answer. Notice the difference between Option B and the other options.

(8)   (B) The former is a mollusk with a shell, while the latter is a human body tissue.

This is another pair of homophones. One is an animal, a mollusk with shell, while the other is a human body tissue.

(9)   (A) The former is a vegetable while the latter is a hole where water can escape accidentally.

Leek is a type of edible vegetable. On the other hand, a *leak* is a hole where water can escape accidentally.

(10)   (C) Accessories

Considering all the options, only Option C spells *accessories* correctly. The other options have incorrect spellings.

(11)   (C) Secretery

While other words are spelled correctly, *secretery* is not the right spelling of the word *secretary*. Hence, it is the misspelled word in the sentence.

(12)   (A) Wail

Considering the context, *wail* is a misspelled word. The sentence is obviously talking about an aquatic animal, the whale. The similar sound may be responsible for the mix-up.

(13)   (C) What a miss!

This is an exclamatory sentence. The rule of thumb stipulates that such words or phrases should end with an exclamation mark (!). Hence, "What a miss!" is the correct sentence.

(14)   (B) There are five boys in the classroom.

If you are familiar with punctuation marks, especially the apostrophe, you will understand why the other options are wrong. An apostrophe is a punctuation mark that shows possession or ownership. Nothing in the sentence indicates possession. Rather, the word *five* indicates a plural noun. Thus, all the sentences that contain an apostrophe are incorrect.

(15)   (B) I love three things: movies, books, and music.

The ellipsis in the original sentence is inappropriate. More so, the quotation marks in Option A are unnecessary since it is not quoted speech. The period before the list in Option C makes the list an incomplete sentence. The comma before the list in Option D renders it incorrect.

(16)   (C) *Bite* means "to use teeth to tear something apart," while *byte* is a measurement unit of digital information.

Byte and *bite* are often confused. *Bite* means "to use teeth to tear something apart." *Byte*, on the other hand, is a measurement unit of digital information (e.g., 100 bytes of data is stored in the file).

(17)   (B) The cat ate the source.

Option B is the odd member of the list. *Sauce* is replaced with *source*, invalidating Option B. Options A, C, and D are correct sentences devoid of any type of error.

(18)   (C) Soulely

Soulely is the only error in the sentence. The other words are devoid of spelling errors. The correct spelling is *solely*.

(19)   (B) She was injured from the waist down.

Waste in Option A is inappropriate since it means "garbage." The appropriate word is *waist*, the part of the body round your middle. Since *injury* is a noun, those sentences where it appears do not have a verb and are incorrect. This invalidates options C and D.

(20)   (D) A question mark is missing from the sentence.

This is an interrogative sentence. Thus, it must end with a question mark. However, as can be seen, the question mark is missing. An apostrophe, a colon, or an exclamation mark would not fit here.

Incident Report Writing Test 3: Answers & Explanations

(1)   (B) An informer who refuses to reveal their identity

In this context, an anonymous caller is someone who notified the police of an attempted bank robbery without revealing their identity, obviously for security reasons.

(2)   (D) 15 minutes

The police headquarters received a distress call from an anonymous caller at about 0800 hours. In a swift response to the call, a five-man squad was dispatched to the bank. The team arrived at the scene at 0815 hours. That was some 15 minutes later.

(3)   (B) 30 minutes

According to the passage, the face-off lasted some 30 minutes, during which time four of the robbers were arrested and their leader managed to escape.

(4)   (A) He is tall and muscular.

As indicated in the report, the escaped robber is tall and muscular. The passage specifically states that the suspect is a middle-aged man, about 6 feet tall. He is a muscular African American and weighs approximately 240 lbs.

(5)   (B) Long years of alcohol and drug use

His bloodshot eyes are indicative of regular hard drugs or alcohol use. Addiction to these substances has undoubtedly affected the color of his eyeballs.

(6)   (A) Self-important

The suspect takes pride in his appearance, so this is the most appropriate answer.

(7)   (A) Unmistakable

The report describes the escaped robber as walking with a distinct gait. That is an unmistakable attribute. Supporting this, the passage claims that the gait will make the robber stand out from a crowd.

(8)   (A) His expensive shirt and gold-colored wristwatch

As of the time of his flight, he wore an expensive shirt over bright-colored slacks. He had a blue scarf tied around his neck, matching the color of his bracelets. He had three rings on each hand and a gold-colored wristwatch to match the color of the rings. This outfit suggests he is wealthy and leads an opulent life.

(9)   (C) Their collaboration with the bank's security personnel

Working in collaboration with the bank's security, the police foiled the attempted robbery. The joint efforts of the police and the bank's security personnel gave them an advantage in this situation.

(10)   (A) He made a significant contribution to the victory.

The anonymous caller contributed to the operation's success. If he had not provided the prompt tip-off, the police may have arrived at the robbery scene later and the robbers may have had a successful raid.

Test 4

Mathematics Test 4: Questions

(1)   Calculate 50% of $30,000

(A) $12,000

(B) $10,000

(C) $15,000

(D) $18,000

(2)   What is the average of $12,000, $10,000, and $23,000?

(A) $17,000

(B) $15,000

(C) $18,000

(D) $11,000

(3)   It is estimated that it will take a driver three hours to cover 210 miles. What is the driver's average speed?

(A)   80 miles per hour

(B)   70 miles per hour

(C)   90 miles per hour

(D)   85 miles per hour

(4)   The crime rates in three states over a period of two years are 23,100, 2,300, and 12,700. Find the average yearly crime rate for all three states combined.

(A)   19,050

(B)   11,667

(C)   12,677

(D)   13,667

(5)   An investigation into increasing crime rates in a county revealed three major causes: poverty, peer pressure, and drug abuse. If peer pressure is responsible for 2/3 of the crimes in the county, how many out of the 2,700 crime incidents in the county are caused by peer pressure?

(A)   1,500

(B)   2,100

(C)   1,800

(D)   1,750

(6)   What is the number of crimes caused by poverty and drug abuse according to the stats in the question above?

(A)   1,200

(B)   1,450

(C)   1,300

(D)   900

(7)   From available records, only a third of kidnapping-related cases in Chicago were kidnaps successfully carried out. If 1,200 kidnapping cases were recorded in 2017, how many kidnapping-related cases were recorded in that year?

(A)   3,800

(B)   3,500

(C)   3,600

(D)   3,000

(8)   The local court recorded 570 successful divorce cases in a community in 2005. If only a half of the divorce cases filed were successful, how many divorces cases were filed?

(A)   1,150

(B)   285

(C)   1,120

(D)   1,140

(9)   A burglary victim reportedly lost a $125.50 wristwatch, $500 worth of pants, and a $520 mobile phone to the theft. What was the total value lost?

(A) $1,245.50

(B) $1,240.50

(C) $1,255.50

(D) $1,145.50

(10)   Seven out of the 10 armed robbery suspects arraigned last month were sentenced to death. What percentage of the suspects escaped the death sentence?

(A)   50%

(B)   30%

(C)   40%

(D)   20%

(11)   An officer makes three trips to a city every week. How many trips does he make to the city in two years?

(A)   310

(B)   315

(C)   312

(D)   320

(12)   What percentage of $3,500 is $1,750?

(A)   45%

(B)   48%

(C)   40%

(D)   50%

(13)   After his arrest for fraud, a fraudster returned 50% of his fraudulent income. If he returned $35,000, how much did he fraudulently steal?

(A) $50,000

(B) $70,000

(C) $75,000

(D) $90,000

(14)   What is the capacity of a prison if the 1,200 inmates make up just 1/3 of its full capacity?

(A)   3,500

(B)   3,000

(C)   3,600

(D)   5,500

(15)   What fraction of 30,000 inmates is 20,000 inmates?

(A)   2/3

(B)   2/5

(C)   2/7

(D)   2/9

(16)   When checking the inventory of his store, a store owner discovered that 1/10 of his female fashion accessories have been stolen. If he counted 2,700 female fashion accessories, how many accessories were there before the theft?

(A)   3,500

(B)   3,000

(C)   3,700

(D)   4,500

(17)   A stolen vehicle was sold for 80% of its actual price. If the vehicle was sold for $2,400, what is its actual price?

(A) $5,000

(B) $4,000

(C) $6,500

(D) $3,000

(18)   For a bank, the average yearly amount of money lost to robbery over five years is $800,000. How much did the bank lose over that period?

(A) $7 million

(B) $8 million

(C) $5 million

(D) $4 million

(19) Find the difference between $56,000 and $23,000.

(A) $33,000

(B) $35,000

(C) $32,000

(D) $45,000

(20) Three criminals were separately charged $23,000, $12,000, and $10,000. What was the average amount charged?

(A) $15,000

(B) $45,000

(C) $35,000

(D) $22,500

Reading Test 4: Passages

Passage 7: How Dangerous Is Organized Crime?

Organized crime refers to the setting up of a centralized organization with the primary aim of engaging in criminal and illegal activities. Such organizations engage in illegal activities that range from robbery to cargo theft, kidnapping to ransom, and other vices such as prostitution, usury, drugs, and gambling.

Although they earn their income from illegitimate businesses, these criminals sometimes invest in legitimate businesses, such as loan companies, tourism, and other enterprises, to give their activities a legal backing. The loan companies charge exorbitant interests and forcefully collect their money through violence and threats from defaulting borrowers.

By funding gambling organizations, they also promote all forms of gambling, such as lotto and online casino, across the country. They thereby contribute to the increasing gambling rates among our youth. Thanks to their wealth, organized syndicates can afford to establish a wide range of gambling businesses and attract the right customers to keep their gambling business growing.

The brains behind organized crime do not limit their activities to businesses only. They also wield some power in the political sector, where they can use proceeds of their illicit businesses to gain political power and influence any arm of the government.

You may be wondering why organized criminals thrive in the United States in spite of the government's efforts to rid the country of bad elements. Well, their success is attributed to their modus operandi. At the top of an organized crime syndicate is a leader who has the power of life and death. Their members do not have the luxury of pulling out of such syndicates, even if they desire to come clean and lead an honest life. Such repentant criminals will be dealt with mercilessly to serve as a deterrent to others who may be nursing similar thoughts. It is not unheard of for former members of organized crime groups to be eliminated for daring to turn their backs on such groups.

Another contributing factor to its popularity in the United States is people's attitude toward organized crime. Many people believe that organized crime activities are not immoral and that they do not hurt their victims or negatively affect society. They consider it a legitimate source of livelihood for some people. It follows that they consider the government's efforts to stamp them out as nothing more than misplaced priorities. Some are of the opinion that law enforcement agencies should be tolerant of these syndicates.

It is safe to say that organized crime is showing no sign of slowing down in the United States. The multibillion-dollar industry is a great threat to both the US government and its citizens, for its multifarious activities have both political and economic impacts on the country.

Passage 8: The Role of Social Media in Identity Theft

The increasing rate of identity theft across the globe is a major source of concern for security-conscious individuals and the government. The Consumer Sentinel Network Data Book reported that over 167,000 victims of identity theft had their identities used to open fraudulent credit card accounts in 2019.

If that sounds bad, a study by Javelin Strategy & Research, titled "2019 Identity Fraud Study," reported that 16.7 million and 14.4 million people were victims of identity theft in 2017 and 2018, respectively. This highlights the prevalence of this crime across the United States. What role has social media played in the proliferation of identity theft?

Social media provides identity thieves with the platform they need to harvest their victims' information and use this for any form of crime. For instance, if you intentionally or accidentally post your account details on your social media account, you expose yourself to the danger of identity theft. A cybercriminal may steal the information and hurt you or others with it. Such a costly mistake may not only cost you your identity, but you will also bear the consequences of whatever crime is perpetrated through your identity. Imagine losing your entire savings to a criminal, thanks to your information at their disposal.

You also put yourself at risk of identity theft when you accept friend requests or connections from unknown social media users. That seemingly harmless "friend" you just added to your list may be a cybercriminal in disguise. They may take a clue from your social media posts to guess your password and other pieces of information. Thus, you must watch your social media activities.

Some expose themselves to identity theft when they update their social media accounts with confidential or sensitive information such as going on a vacation for days or weeks. A potential criminal may take advantage of your absence to ransack your home and steal documents that may contain your personal information.

Recently, a musician was assassinated shortly after updating his Instagram story with his current location. That update made it easier for his killers to locate him.

Reading Test 4: Questions

(1)   Define organized crime.

(A)   The setting up of a centralized body for illegal and criminal activities

(B)   The setting up of a decentralized body for illegal and criminal activities

(C)   The setting up of a centralized body for illegal activities only

(D)   The setting up of a centralized body for criminal activities only

(2)   Which of the following is not a part of organized crime?

(A)   Prostitution

(B)   Armed robbery

(C)   Drug pushing

(D)   None of the above

(3)   Which of the words below can replace *exorbitant*?

(A)   Inexpensive

(B)   Inconsiderate

(C)   High

(D)   Affordable

(4)   How do organized criminals cover up their activities?

(A)   They employ experts to cover their tracks.

(B)   They invest in legitimate businesses to give their illegal activities a legal appearance.

(C)   They pay their taxes when due.

(D)   They do not get involved in anti-government activities.

(5)   How do organized crime organizations promote gambling?

(A)   By giving individuals who are interested in gambling enough money to kickstart their gambling career

(B)   By establishing an array of gambling businesses

(C)   By employing competent hands to manage their businesses

(D)   All of the above.

(6)   Organized crime groups limit their activities to the business sector only. True or false?

(A)   Not really

(B)   True

(C)   False

(D)   Sometimes

(7)   Define *modus operandi.*

(A)   Hierarchy of operation

(B)   Method of operation

(C)   Tools of operation

(D)   Extent of operation

(8)   According to the passage, what does *have the power of life and death* mean?

(A)   They can decide who lives or dies.

(B)   They know what it takes to die or be alive.

(C)   They give their members the luxury of choosing between life and death.

(D)   They live life on the edge without giving a second thought to life and death.

(9)   What is the connection between people's attitude toward organized crime and its success in the United States?

(A)   Its success is dependent on people's attitude toward it.

(B)   Its success is independent of people's attitude toward it.

(C)   People turn a blind eye toward organized crime.

(D)   None of the above.

(10)   What from the passage indicates that some people are tolerant of organized crime?

(A)   Some people believe it should not be eradicated.

(B)   Some people are advocating more tolerance of organized crime.

(C)   None of the above.

(D)   Both A and B.

(11)   Why are some people sympathetic toward organized criminals?

(A)   They believe that such criminals are not hurting their victims.

(B)   They believe that such crimes are totally harmless.

(C)   They believe that organized crime is the source of livelihood for many people.

(D)   All of the above.

(12)   Which word can replace *multifarious* from the list below?

(A)   Manifold

(B)   Uniform

(C)   Multitasking

(D)   Multiple

(13)   Why are people concerned about identity theft?

(A)   It is an increasing security challenge.

(B)   They are curious to know its gravity.

(C)   None of the above.

(D)   Both A and B.

(14)   How prevalent is identity theft in the United States?

(A)   Hundreds of thousands of people are victims of identity theft in the United States each year.

(B)   Hundreds of millions of people are victims of identity theft in the United States each year.

(C)   Tens of millions of people are victims of identity theft in the United States each year.

(D)   Millions of people are victims of identity theft in the United States each year.

(15)   What is social media's role in identity theft?

(A)   Identity thieves harvest personal information for their nefarious activities through their victims' social media posts and updates.

(B)   Social media platforms willingly provide personal details of their users to potential identity thieves.

(C)   Social media is the only platform through which victims become prey to identity theft.

(D)   Social media does not play a significant role in identity theft.

(16)   Why is identity theft dangerous?

(A)   A stolen identity may be used for criminal activities.

(B)   The victim may have to create another social media account to protect their identity.

(C)   Identity theft may cause physical pain to the victim.

(D)   The danger of identity theft is a function of several factors.

(17)   What is the danger of accepting a friend request from a random individual on social media?

(A)   It increases the chances of losing one's privacy.

(B)   It increases the chances of losing one's identity.

(C)   None of the above.

(D)   Both A and B.

(18)   How do some people make themselves vulnerable to identity theft?

(A)   They post confidential information on their social media accounts.

(B)   They use social media irregularly.

(C)   They cannot do without using social media.

(D)   They use social media for business only.

(19)   If Kenny accidentally posts his transaction details on social media, what risk does he run?

(A)   The risk of exposing his bank details

(B)   The risk of having his identity stolen

(C)   The risk of losing his money

(D)   All of the above

(20)   How can you fortify yourself against identity theft?

(A)   By not using social media at all

(B)   By using social media at specific times of the day

(C)   By watching your online activities when using social media

(D)   None of the above

(21)   What does *costly mistake* refer to in the passage?

(A)   To making your personal information public knowledge on social media

(B)   To the death of the musician.

(C)   To losing your identity to a cybercriminal

(D)   To using social media for personal purposes

(22)   What does *in disguise* mean in the passage?

(A)   Pretending to be your friend

(B)   Pretending to be someone else

(C)   Pretending to have your welfare at heart

(D)   Doing their best to steal your identity

(23)   Who suffers the effects of identity theft?

(A)   The individual whose identity is stolen

(B)   Friends of the individual whose identity is stolen

(C)   Family members of the individual whose identity is stolen

(D)   All of the above

(24)   What does *seemingly harmless* mean in the passage?

(A)   Someone who pretends to love you but hates you

(B)   Someone who pretends to hate you but loves you

(C)   Someone who pretends to be your friend but really is your enemy

(D)   Someone who is really interested in your welfare

(25)   According to the passage, what does *at their disposal* mean?

(A)   Readily available

(B)   Difficult to come by

(C)   Easily bought

(D)   Already on hand

Grammar Test 4: Questions

(1)   Choose the synonym for the underlined word in the following sentence. *The man's <u>propensity</u> for crime is legendary.*

(A)   Inclination

(B)   Hatred

(C)   Advocacy

(D)   All of the above

(2)   What is the opposite of the underlined word in the following sentence? *She is a <u>shrewd</u> woman.*

(A)   Hardworking

(B)   Unwise

(C)   Educated

(D)   Intelligent

(3)   *The versatile entertainer is not only a good dancer, he is also a good singer.* What does *versatile* mean in the preceding sentence?

(A)   All-around

(B)   Sympathetic

(C)   Great

(D)   Popular

(4)   What can you replace insubordinate with in the following sentence? *The employee was insubordinate.*

(A)   Disobedient

(B)   Supportive

(C)   Respectful

(D)   All of the above

(5)   Differentiate between *wheel* and *will*.

(A)   A will is a part of an object that enables it to move freely, while a wheel is a written document passing a deceased's property to his family or others.

(B)   A wheel is a part of an object that enables it to rotate about an axis, while a will is a written document passing a deceased's property to his family or others.

(C)   A wheel is a part of an object that enables it to move freely, while a will is a written document passing a deceased's property to his family or others.

(D)   A will is a part of an object that enables it to rotate about an axis, while a wheel is a written document passing a deceased's property to his family or others.

(6)   What is the difference between *you* and *ewe*?

(A)   *You* is a pronoun, whereas *ewe* is an adverb.

(B)   *You* is a pronoun, whereas *ewe* is a noun.

(C)   *You* is an adverb, whereas *ewe* is a verb.

(D)   *You* is an adjective, whereas *ewe* is a coordinating conjunction.

(7) Identify the misspelled word in the following sentence. *He recieved the assorted items from the delivery man.*

(A) Assorted

(B) Delivery

(C) Recieved

(D) Items

(8) Identify the wrong sentence from the sentences below.

(A) The boy's attitude to work is nothing to right home about.

(B) She is extremely choosy.

(C) What a lovely delivery from the renowned motivational speaker!

(D) The little girl is in a world of her own.

(9) Identify the correct option below. How did he feel about the elimination?

(A) He considers it a humiliating experience.

(B) He considers it a humiliation experience.

(C) He consideres it a humiliating experience.

(D) He consideres it a humiliation experience.

(10)   Differentiate between *isle* and *aisle*.

(A)   An aisle is the passage between two rows of seats, whereas an isle is a small island.

(B)   An isle is the passage between two rows of seats, whereas an aisle is a small island.

(C)   An aisle is the passage between three rows of seats, whereas an isle is a small island.

(D)   An isle is the passage between three rows of seats, whereas an isle is a small island.

(11)   What is the difference between *there* and *their*?

(A)   *There* means "at that place," while *their* means "belonging to the person or thing mentioned."

(B)   *Their* means "at that place," while *there* means "belonging to the person or thing mentioned."

(C)   *There* means "at this place," while *their* means "belonging to the person or thing mentioned."

(D)   *There* means "at that place," while *their* means "belonging to us."

(12)   Identify the correct sentence from the list below.

(A)   She is a replica of her mother.

(B)   She is a replicer of her mother.

(C)   She is a repllica of her mother.

(D)   She is a replicca of her mother.

(13)   Identify the correct sentence from the list of sentences below.

(A)   There is a clear distinction between the two footballers.

(B)   Nothing is more satisfying than having a credible sauce of income.

(C)   The school's principle will be around before noon.

(D)   The minimum requirement for admittance.

(14)   What is the distinction between *it's* and *its*?

(A)   *It's* is a contracted form of *it is* or it has, while *its* is a possessive adjective.

(B)   *Its* is a contracted form of *it is* or it has, while *it's* is a possessive adjective.

(C)   *It's* is a contracted form of *it is*, while *its* is a contracted form of *it has*.

(D)   *It's* is a contracted form of *it has*, while *its* is a contracted form of *it is*.

(15)   Rewrite the following sentence. *The boy and his mother are member of the group.*

(A)   The boy, his mother, are members of the group.

(B)   The boy and his mother are members of the group.

(C)   The boy and his mother is a member of the group.

(D)   The boy and his mother are a member of the group.

(16)   What is the missing punctuation mark in the following sentence? The aged woman who came visiting last month is dead.

(A)   An apostrophe.

(B)   Parentheses.

(C)   A period.

(D)   An exclamation mark.

(17)   *The footballers, alongside their coach, are to blame for the loss.* Rewrite the previous sentence.

(A)   The sentence is error-free.

(B)   The footballers, together with their coach, are to blame for the loss.

(C)   The footballers, as well as their coach, are to blame for the loss.

(D)   The footballers, alongside their coach, is to blame for the loss.

(18)   Rewrite the following sentence. *Mathematics make the world go round.*

(A)   Mathematics make the world go round.

(B)   Mathematic make the world go round.

(C)   Mathematics makes the world go round.

(D)   Mathematic makes the world go round.

(19)   Rewrite the following sentence. *Nobody love failure, we all love success.*

(A)   Nobody love failure because we all love success.

(B)   Nobody love failure but everybody love success.

(C)   Nobody loves failure; we all love success.

(D)   The sentence is error-free.

(20)   Which of the following sentences is correct?

(A)   A five-man committee was set up to review the fraud incident.

(B)   A five-men committee was set up to review the fraud incident.

(C)   A five men committee was set up to review the fraud incident.

(D)   A five man committee was set up to review the fraud incident.

Incident Report Writing Test 4

<u>Report Sample 4</u>

Incident No: DRMO/2000/5/12546

Incident: Arson

Address: Road 8, House 10, Bellview Estate, Texas

Date of Call: July 19, 2020

Time of Call: 0825 hours

While on patrol on July 19, 2020, we received a distress call notifying us of a suspected arson case at Road 8, Bellview Estate, Texas. We arrived at the scene of the incident at exactly 0830 hours, two minutes after the fire service, who had already put the fire out without allowing it to do much damage to the building.

According to an eyewitness report, a teenage girl about 5 feet and 5 inches tall was seen crossing the road to the bungalow that she eventually set on fire. She reportedly had a backpack, apparently containing the tools she used to commit the crime.

Before we arrived at the scene, the suspect reportedly disappeared into thin air, leaving her backpack behind some feet away from the burning house. According to CCTV camera footage, the suspect, a brunette, is in her mid-teens. She is slimly built with an athletic physique, suggesting that she is either a sportsperson or into fitness.

Her oblong face and thin lips give her a distinct appearance. She has a cat tattoo on her left arm as revealed by the short-sleeve top she wore over black sportswear. She wore a pair of Nike sports shoes and a medal around her neck.

The white female has a pair of blue eyes and a pair of protruding ears. Her athleticism is also reflected in how she walks. She walks upright and smartly, signaling her youthfulness and commitment to workouts. The footage showed her using the back exit to escape after starting the fire in the living room.

Her personal details have been entered into our database as we investigate the motive behind the arson as well as work to identify and apprehend the suspect.

Incident Report Writing Test 4: Questions

(1)   What impression about the arsonist was given by her physique?

(A)   She is passionate about physical fitness.

(B)   She is in the military.

(C)   She loves wearing sportswear.

(D)   She is dedicated to crime.

(2)   When did the fire service arrive at the crime scene?

(A)   0828 hours

(B)   0928 hours

(C)   0800 hours

(D)   0830 hours

(3)   Guess the suspect's age.

(A)   Between 12 and 18 years old

(B)   Between 15 and 17 years old

(C)   Between 15 and 20 years old

(D)   Between 25 and 30 years old

(4)   What does *disappeared into thin air* mean?

(A)   The suspect literally disappeared.

(B)   The suspect's whereabouts were unknown.

(C)   The suspect leveraged the power of natural elements for her disappearance.

(D)   The suspect went into the air.

(5)   What can you say about the suspect's hair?

(A)   She has golden hair.

(B)   She has dark brown hair.

(C)   She has grey hair.

(D)   She has blue and green hair.

(6)   What can you deduce from the suspect's gait?

(A)   She is athletic and fit.

(B)   She is sloppy and unkempt.

(C)   She walks with a sloppy gait.

(D)   None of the above.

(7)   How did the suspect escape the bungalow?

(A)   Through the laundry room

(B)   Through the visitors' room

(C)   Through the fire exit

(D)   Through the back exit

(8)   Summarize the suspect's appearance.

(A)   She's youthful and fit.

(B)   She is scary and mean.

(C)   She is accommodating and callous.

(D)   None of the above.

(9)   Appraise the police's response to the distress call.

(A)   They responded swiftly to the distress call.

(B)   Their response to the distress call was nothing to write home about.

(C)   They displayed a measure of nonchalance toward the incident.

(D)   They took their time to respond to the distress call.

(10)   Why were the suspect's details entered into the police's database?

(A)   To enable them to identify and apprehend the suspect

(B)   To enable them to identify the motive behind the crime

(C)   None of the above

(D)   Both A and B

Mathematics Test 4: Answers& Explanations

(1)   (C) $15,000

50% of $30,000 = (50/100) × 30,000

= 0.5 × 30,000 = 15,000

Hence, $15,000 is 50% of $30,000.

(2)   (B) $15,000

Total sum of money = $12,000 + $10,000 + $23,000 = $45,000

Average = total amount of money/how many amounts there are

Average = $45,000/3 = $15,000

Hence, the average of $12,000, $10,000, and $23,000 is $15,000.

(3)   (B) 70 miles per hour

Distance covered: 210 miles

Time taken: 3 hours

Average speed: distance covered/time taken

= 210 miles/3 hours = 70 miles per hour

The driver's average speed is 70 miles per hour.

(4)   (A) 19,050

Number of reported crimes in State 1: 23,100

Number of reported crimes in State 2: 2,300

Number of reported crimes in State 3: 12,700

Total crime rate = reported crime in state 1 + reported crime in state 2 + reported crime in state 3

= 23,100 + 2,300 + 12,700 = 38,100

Average crime rate = total crime rate/number of years

= 38,100/2 = 19,050

Hence, the average crime rate for the three states over one year is 19,050 cases.

(5)   (C) 1,800

Number of reported crimes: 2,700

Fraction of crimes caused by peer pressure: 2/3

Number of crimes caused by peer pressure = fraction of crimes caused by peer pressure × number of reported crimes

= 2/3 × 2,700

= 5,400/3

= 1,800

Hence, peer pressure is responsible for 1,800 of the reported crimes.

(6)   (D) 900

Since peer pressure is responsible for 1,800 of the crime incidents, poverty and drugs are responsible for the remaining incidents.

Total number of crime incidents: 2,700

Number of crimes ascribed to peer pressure: 1,800

Total number of crimes ascribed to poverty and drugs = total number of crime incidents – number of crimes ascribed to peer pressure

= 2,700 crimes – 1,800 crimes = 900 crimes

Hence, poverty and drug abuse are responsible for 900 crimes.

(7)   (C) 3,600

Number of successful kidnapping cases: 1,200

Fraction that are kidnapping cases: 1/3

Number of kidnapping-related cases = number of successful kidnapping cases × 3

= 1,200 cases × 3 = 3,600 cases

3,600 kidnapping-related cases were reported in 2017.

(8)   (D) 1,140

Number of successful divorce cases: 570

Fraction of successful divorce cases: ½

Total number of filed divorce cases = number of successful divorce cases × 2

= 570 cases × 2 = 1,140 cases

Hence, 1,140 divorce cases were filed.

(9)   (D) $1,145.50

Value of wristwatch: $125.50

Value of pants: $500

Value of mobile phone: $520

Total value lost = value of wristwatch + value of pants + value of mobile phone

= $125.50 + $500 + $520 = $1,145.50

So the total value lost was $1,145.50.

(10)   (B) 30%

Number of arraigned suspects: 10

Number of suspects given the death sentence: 7

Number of suspects not given death sentence = number of arraigned suspects − number of suspects given the death sentence.

= 10 suspects − 7 suspects = 3 suspects

Percentage of suspects who escaped the death sentence = (number of suspects who escaped the death sentence/number of suspects arraigned) × 100

= (3/10) × 100

= 0.3 × 100

= 30

Hence, 30% of the suspects escaped the death sentence.

(11)   (C) 312

Number of trips per week: 3

Number of years: 2

Number of weeks per year: 52.

Number of weeks in 2 years = 52 weeks × 2 = 104 weeks

Number of trips in 2 years = number of trips per week × number of weeks in 2 years

= 3 trips × 104 = 312 trips.

The officer made 312 trips to the city in 2 years.

(12)   (D) 50%

Total amount: $3,500

Part amount: $1,750

Percentage of fraction to original amount = (part amount/total amount) × 100

= ($1,750/$3,500) × 100

Divide through to simplify the fraction.

= (175/350) × 100

= (35/70) × 100

= (5/10) × 100

= 0.5 × 100

= 50

Thus, $1,750 is 50% of $3,500.

(13)   (B) $70,000

Amount returned: $35,000

Fraction of amount returned: 50% or ½

Actual amount = amount returned × 2

= $35,000 × 2 = $70,000

He fraudulently stole $70,000.

(14)   (C) 3,600

Number of inmates: 1,200

Fraction of prison capacity: 1/3

Actual capacity = number of inmates × 3

= 1,200 inmates × 3

= 3,600 inmates

The capacity of the prison is 3,600 inmates.

(15)   (A) 2/3

Number of inmates: 30,000

Section of inmates: 20,000

Fraction of section to actual number of inmates = 20,000/30,000

Divide through by 10,000.

20,000/30,000 = 2/3

Thus, 20,000 inmates is 2/3 of 30,000 inmates.

(16)   (B) 3,000

Number of accessories left: 2,700

Fraction of stolen accessories: 1/10

Fraction of accessories left = 1 − 1/10 = 9/10

Let x be the number of accessories before the theft.

9/10 = 2,700/x

9 × x = 10 × 2,700

9x = 27,000

Divide through by 9.

x = 3,000

Hence, the shop owner had 3,000 female fashion accessories before the theft.

(17)   (D) $3,000

Vehicle's selling price: $2,400

Percentage of original price: 80% or 8/10

Original price = (selling price/8) × 10

= ($2,400/8) × 10

= $300 × 10

= $3,000

Hence, the vehicle's original price is $3,000.

(18)   (D) $4 million

Number of years: 5

Total money lost = average amount of money lost per year × number of years

= $800,000 × 5 years = $4,000,000

Hence, the bank lost $4 million over that period.

(19)   (A) The difference is $33,000.

Bigger number: $56,000

Smaller number: $23,000

Difference = bigger number − smaller number

= $56,000 − $23,000 = $33,000

Thus, the difference between $56,000 and $23,000 is $33,000.

(20)   (A) $15,000

First criminal charge: $23,000

Second criminal charge: $12,000

Third criminal charge: $10,000

Sum = first criminal charge + second criminal charge + third criminal charge

= $23,000 + $12,000 + $10,000 = $45,000

Average = sum/number of criminals

= $45,000/3 = $15,000

Hence, they were charged $15,000 on average.

Reading Test 4: Answers & Explanations

(1)   (A) The setting up of a centralized body for illegal and criminal activities

Organized crime refers to the setting up of a centralized organization with the primary aim of engaging in criminal and illegal activities. Such organizations engage in illegal activities that range from robbery to cargo theft, kidnapping to ransom, and other vices such as prostitution, usury, drugs, and gambling.

(2)   (D) None of the above

Organized crime organizations have interests in virtually all types of illegal business, from drugs to prostitution, terrorism to armed robbery—every sort of illegal businesses you can think of.

(3)   (C) High

From the list, only *high* can replace *exorbitant*. The passage explains that although some organized crime organizations invest in seemingly legitimate loan companies, they charge interest rates that are very high.

(4)   (B) They invest in legitimate businesses to give their illegal activities a legal appearance.

Although they earn their income from illegitimate businesses, they sometimes invest in legitimate businesses, such as loan companies, tourism, and other businesses, to give their activities a legal backing.

(5)   (B) By establishing an array of gambling businesses

They promote gambling by investing in all types of gambling businesses. By funding gambling organizations, they promote all forms of gambling, such as lotto and online casino, across the country.

(6)   (C) False

The brains behind organized crime do not limit their activities to businesses only. They also wield some power in the political sector, where they can use proceeds of their illicit businesses to gain political power and influence any arm of the government.

(7)   (B) Method of operation

Modus operandi means "a particular way of doing something." According to the passage, it refers to the ways organized crime groups carry out their criminal activity as the secret behind their success.

(8)   (A) They can decide who lives or dies.

The members of organized crime gangs do not have the luxury of pulling out of such syndicates, even if they desire to come clean and lead an honest life. Such repentant criminals will be dealt with mercilessly to serve as deterrent to others who may be nursing similar thoughts.

(9)   (A) Its success is dependent on people's attitude toward it.

Another contributing factor to its popularity in the United States is people's attitude toward organized crime. Many people believe that the organized crime activities are not immoral and do not have negative effects on society. They consider it a legitimate source of livelihood for some people.

(10)   (D) Both A and B.

The passage states how "They consider [organized crime] a legitimate source of livelihood for some people. It follows that they consider the government's efforts to stamp them out as nothing more than misplaced priorities. Some are of the opinion that law enforcement agencies should be tolerant of these syndicates."

(11)   (D) All of the above.

Some people are sympathetic toward organized criminals because they believe that such criminals are not hurting their victims. They consider them to be harmless and just trying to earn a living.

(12)   (A) Manifold

Multifarious can be replaced with *manifold* in the passage. This is because *multifarious* means "having many varied parts or aspects" in reference to the several businesses that organized crime organizations invest in.

(13)   (A) It is an increasing security challenge.

The increasing rate of identity theft across the globe is a major source of concern for security-conscious individuals and the government. Statistics show that millions of people have become victims of identity theft over the years.

(14)   (C) Tens of millions of people are victims of identity theft in the United States each year.

A study by Javelin Strategy & Research, titled "2019 Identity Fraud Study," reported that 16.7 million and 14.4 million people were victims of identity theft in 2017 and 2018, respectively. This highlights the prevalence of this crime across the United States.

(15)   (A) Identity thieves harvest personal information for their nefarious activities through their victims' social media posts and updates.

If you intentionally or accidentally post your account details on your social media account, you expose yourself to the danger of identity theft. A cybercriminal may steal the information and hurt you or others with it.

(16)   (A) A stolen identity may be used for criminal activities.

Identity thieves use the stolen identity for criminal activities. The Consumer Sentinel Network Data Book reported that over 167,000 victims of identity theft had their identities used to open fraudulent credit card accounts in 2019.

(17)   (B) It increases the chances of losing one's identity.

You put yourself at risk of identity theft when you accept friend requests or connections from unknown social media users. That seemingly harmless "friend" you just added to your list may be a cybercriminal in disguise. They may gather sensitive information from your online activities.

(18)   (A) They post confidential information on their social media accounts.

Some expose themselves to identity theft when they update their social media accounts with confidential or sensitive information, such as going on a vacation for days or weeks. A potential criminal may take advantage of their absence to ransack their home.

(19)   (D) All of the above

Kenny runs several risks if he accidentally posts his transaction details on social media. He may expose his bank details, have his identity stolen, and lose his savings to cyber criminals, all thanks to this costly mistake.

(20)   (C) By watching your online activities when using social media

While it may be impractical to stop using social media or restrict its usage to some specific times of the day, you can watch your online activities and put some measures in place to make yourself less vulnerable to attacks.

(21)   (A) To making your personal information public knowledge on social media

The *costly mistake* in the context of the passage refers to people intentionally or accidentally leaving their confidential information on social media, thus making it easier for criminals to gain access to such information.

(22)   (B) Pretending to be someone else

Some people pose as someone else on social media platforms to lure and deceive unwary prey. While posing as a friend, they are mostly scammers or engaging in other related criminal activities.

(23)   (D) All of the above

Sadly, not only the direct victims of identity theft suffer the consequences. Their friends and family members may suffer alongside them. For instance, a stolen identity may be used to defraud friends and family members of the identity theft victim. Everyone around the victim could be a potential target.

(24)   (C) Someone who pretends to be your friend but really is your enemy

In the context of the passage, the seemingly harmless "friend" may actually be preying on you, looking for any opportunity to showcase their criminal tendencies. Hence, while they pretend to be your friend, they are actually your enemy.

(25)   (A) It means readily available.

At their disposal means "it is readily available to them." This refers to your personal information they can easily access through your social media activities.

Grammar Test 4: Answers & Explanations

(1)   (A) Inclination

Propensity means "having a natural tendency," and so does *inclination*. Thus, *propensity* and *inclination* are synonyms.

(2)   (B) Unwise

A shrewd person is wise. Hence, the opposite is *unwise*. Therefore, *unwise* is the opposite of the underlined word.

(3)   (A) All-around

A versatile person is someone who can adapt to different activities or functions. In this context, the entertainer can sing as well as dance. Thus, he is an all-around entertainer. Therefore, *all-around* can replace *versatile* in the sentence.

(4)   (A) Disobedient

Disobedient can replace *insubordinate* in the sentence. *Insubordination* means "refusal to obey orders." Simply stated, *insubordination* is synonymous with *disobedience*.

(5)   (C) A wheel is a part of an object that enables it to move freely, while a will is a written document passing a deceased's property to his family or others.

Through a will, a deceased can transfer property to the next of kin, a family member, or other people. On the other hand, a wheel is a part of an object that enables the object to move freely. An example is a vehicle's wheels.

(6)   (B) *You* is a pronoun, whereas *ewe* is a noun.

You is a pronoun, while *ewe*, a female sheep, is a noun. Remember that a noun is the name of any person, animal, place, or thing.

(7)   (C) Recieved

Recieved is the only misspelled word in the sentence. The correct spelling is *received*. Note that the *e* comes before the *i*, and not the other way around. Other words are spelled correctly.

(8)   (A) The boy's attitude to work is nothing to right home about.

The correct expression is *nothing to write home about*. When *write* is replaced by *right*, the sentence is flawed.

(9)   (A) He considers it a humiliating experience.

Option A aptly describes how the individual feels without spelling errors. However, using *humiliation* invalidates Option B since it is not an adjective. *Considers* is spelled incorrectly in Options C and D.

(10)   (A) An aisle is the passage between two rows of seats, whereas an isle is a small island.

The homophones *isle* and *aisle* are often mixed up. However, note that while an aisle is the passage between two rows of seats, an isle is a small island. For instance, "He walked down the aisle on his flight to the isle."

(11)   (A) *There* means "at that place," while *their* means "belonging to the person or thing mentioned."

There means "at that place." For instance, "Put it there." Conversely, *their* means "belonging to the person or thing mentioned." For instance, "That is their house over there."

(12)   (A) She is a replica of her mother.

The correct spelling is *replica*. Thus, Option A is the correct sentence. The other options have different incorrect spellings of that specific word.

(13)   (A) There is a clear distinction between the two footballers.

Option A is the only correct option in the list. Option B uses *sauce* as a replacement for *source*, while Option C uses *principle* instead of *principal*. For Option D, *admission* is a more appropriate term than *admittance*. Also, it is not a complete sentence because it does not have a verb.

(14)   (A) *It's* is a contracted for of *it is* or *it has*," while "*its*" is a possessive adjective.

It's and *its* are two commonly confused words. The former is the contracted form of *it is* or "*it has*. For instance, "It has gone" can be rewritten as "It's gone." However, *its* is a possessive adjective. For instance, "Its fur was brown and matted."

(15)   (B) The boy and his mother are members of the group.

This is a test of the concord rules. The subject is *the boy and his mother*. As a plural subject, they attract a plural verb, *are*, and must be represented by singular words. The comma separating *the boy* and *his mother* invalidates Option A. Options C and D contain some singular expressions that invalidate them too.

(16)   (B) Parentheses

The missing punctuation mark in the sentence is parentheses. The sentence can be better written as: "The aged woman (who came visiting last month) is dead." An em dash can serve a similar purpose. The aged woman—who came visiting last month—is dead.

(17)   (A) The sentence is error-free.

A parenthetical statement is a nonessential statement that appears in parentheses in a sentence. The parenthesis rule states that such statements should be ignored when choosing a verb for the sentence. Sometimes, the parenthetical statement may be indicated with commas. The same rule applies.

(18)   (C) Mathematics makes the world go round.

Option C is the correct expression. According to the rule of pluralia tantums, some words, such as school subjects like *mathematics* and *physics*, though ending with an *s*, are treated as singular subjects. Hence, they attract singular verbs, in this case, *makes*. Any option that contains either *mathematic* or *make* is incorrect.

(19)   (C) Nobody loves failure; we all love success.

Nobody is an indefinite pronoun. As such, it is accompanied by singular verbs. Hence, it goes with *loves* in the sentence. Also, these are two independent clauses, so they cannot be joined with a comma. Option C replaces the comma with a semicolon, which makes it grammatically sound. So, "Nobody loves failure; we all love success" is the correct expression.

(20)   (A) A five-man committee was set up to review the fraud incident.

Option A is the correct answer. When *a* precedes a compound adjective, the noun in the compound adjective must be singular. Also, compound adjectives usually contain a hyphen when they come before a noun, which is included in Option A.

Incident Report Writing Test 4: Answers & Explanations

(1)   (A) She is passionate about physical fitness.

According to CCTV footage, the suspect, a brunette, is in her mid-teens. She is slimly built with an athletic physique, suggesting that she is either a sportsperson or into fitness.

(2)   (A) 0828 hours

The police arrived at the scene of the incident at exactly 0830 hours, two minutes after the fire service. Thus, it can be deduced that the fire service arrived at the incident scene at 0828 hours.

(3)   (B) Between 15 and 17 years old

According to CCTV footage, the suspect, a brunette, is in her mid-teens. Thus, she is between 15 and 17 years old.

(4)   (B) The suspect's whereabouts were unknown.

To disappear into thin air suggests that the suspect's whereabouts suddenly could not be established. She escaped from the incident scene without leaving a trace.

(5)   (B) She has dark brown hair.

The report refers to the suspect as a brunette. This indicates that she has dark brown hair, which is the definition of *brunette*.

(6)   (A) She is athletic and fit.

Her athleticism is reflected in how she walks. She walks upright and smartly, signaling her youthfulness and commitment to workouts. Thus, she is athletic and fit.

(7)   (D) Through the back exit.

The footage showed her using the back exit to escape after starting the fire in the living room. That enabled her to avoid running into the law enforcement agents on the ground.

(8)   (A) She is youthful and fit.

Aside from the suspect's athleticism, she is also youthful and fit. The white female has a pair of blue eyes and a pair of protruding ears. She walks upright and smartly, signaling her youthfulness and commitment to workouts.

(9)   (A) They responded swiftly to the distress call.

As shown by the report, the police received the distress call at 0825 hours and arrived at the incident scene at exactly 0830 hours. This was just five minutes after receiving the call. That was a swift response.

(10)   (D) Both A and B

The suspect's details were entered into the database to enable the police to identify the motive behind the arson and identify and apprehend the suspect.

Conclusion

A promising career awaits you on the police force if you can successfully pass the examination. Your performance on the exam depends largely on the extent of your preparation.

The knowledge and tips from this guide should help you feel more prepared for the exam. This is in addition to the questions and answers designed primarily to test your knowledge of the different areas of the exam and equip you for the challenge ahead.

If you study the book thoroughly and routinely implement the tips, you will be sufficiently prepared for the selection test. It is a surefire way to increase your chances of being selected for a career on the police force.

After you have gone through the guide, always test your knowledge using the questions. Review your performance using the answer section and see if you are well prepared for the test or not. If your performance is below par, do not give up. The more earnest effort you put into studying the material and solving the accompanying questions, the better equipped you will be for the examination.

Best of luck!